THE SOOTHSAYINGS OF BAKIS
Goethe's Tragi-Comic Observations on Life, Time, and History

THE SOOTHSAYINGS OF BAKIS

Goethe's Tragi-Comic Observations on Life, Time, and History

By Harold Jantz

The Johns Hopkins Press ⁓ Baltimore

TO ERNST FEISE

Wise Counselor and Good Friend

PREFACE

Even such a small volume as this involves a larger range of indebtedness than one realizes, to critics and perceptive readers, from the past and in the present.

I am most conscious of my indebtedness to good friends and colleagues who have read the manuscript at various stages of its development. Several years ago when it was in first draft, Ernst Feise subjected it to his kind and searching scrutiny and gave me valuable advice, especially on the verse translations. Last June on his eighty-second, and last, birthday I asked his permission to dedicate the little book to him, and it is now inscribed to his memory, which remains fresh and green among all of us who knew him.

TABLE OF CONTENTS

INTRODUCTION

It was no mere coincidence that Goethe wrote the thirty-two quatrains of his " Weissagungen des Bakis " during the stirring critical year 1798. He was watching humanity making its same old errors all over again—this, in the perspective of man's posturings and pretentions, a comic affair, but in the historical results often tragic and depressing. Both the serious and the comic are present in these verses, though it is the comic that has regularly been overlooked.

Just what the verses mean has always been a matter of some doubt. They baffled his contemporaries, and they have continued to baffle those who have read them or commented on them. Even more inaccessible apparently than the meaning of certain parts has been the intent of the whole, and several critics have reached the conclusion that the poet was here indulging in a mere hoax, a mystification without larger meaning or general purpose. Such a conclusion seems unnecessary. Several of the quatrains are as plain-spoken as anyone could wish, and it would be difficult to miss their point. Others yield their secret after small application and modest effort. Only a few (2, 4, 9, 22, 29, 30) have remained deeply obscure to the present day; a few equally difficult ones have been solved correctly during the past century; more, probably, have been "solved" incorrectly or inadequately, largely because they have been interpreted out of context. Back as far as 1847, Heinrich Viehoff in his commentary on Goethe's poems (II, 401–19) had, with perspicacity and good common sense, solved many of them so well that his successors tended less to improve on him than to lapse from his grace and reason. What happens all too often, even in the case of Viehoff, is that though the critic may have the bare, literal solution, he will add an interpretation that goes astray from Goethe's known principles and intentions and breaks down the texture of this work into unrelated fragments. If anyone has caught the Goethean intent of the whole, he has not made it known.

When one does see the quatrains in their own full context and, even more, in the larger context of the poet's imagery in cognate works, a new coherence and consistency, an over-all pattern will be found that makes the single interpretations not only acceptable but convincing. In order to afford the reader easy access to other passages in which Goethe employs similar imagery with similar intent or makes similar reflections, I have added a group of them in an appendix. They will serve to show by comparison how image and intent are related in the poet's mind. Such an appendix is also useful in allowing the observations on each quatrain to remain brief, even very brief, abstaining both from the laborious refutation of other interpretations and also the elaborate, quotation-ridden support of the solution here offered. The aim, then, is not to tell the quatrains what they ought to mean according to a particular attitude or hypothesis but to let Goethe himself tell us what he meant.

If we ask why Goethe presented his comments in such cryptic form, the answer cannot simply be that he enjoyed a good joke and delighted in mystifying his readers a bit. Usually he also had some worthy intent in his jest. What is more, he always played fair with the reader in his mystifications by providing the means for the solution—to him who would take the trouble to look carefully. When the reader sees the point, he can usually see at the same time why the poet had to put it in the form of an enigma: it is generally something that, plainly put, would be passed by as well known and commonplace; when put as a riddle, with a sudden and startling solution, it appears morning-fresh once more to the reader, and he realizes that he did not fully appreciate its significance after all. There is also a deeper reason, as we shall see: only in the form of the cryptic, symbolic utterance could the poet convey tersely the double or multiple meaning he wished to convey. Actually Goethe himself told us the reason. In his "Alexis und Dora" he describes the little drama of a riddle:

> . . . So legt der Dichter ein Rätsel,
> Künstlich mit Worten verschränkt, oft der Versammlung ins Ohr;
> Jeden freuet die seltne, der zierlichen Bilder Verknüpfung,
> Aber noch fehlet das Wort, das die Bedeutung verwahrt;
> Ist es endlich entdeckt, dann heitert sich jedes Gemüt auf
> Und erblickt im Gedicht doppelt erfreulichen Sinn.

> . . . A poet will offer a riddle,
> Cunningly folded in words, unto his listeners' ears.
> Everyone likes the rare connection of delicate pictures,
> Though he still lack the word holding the meaning within.
> Once it is finally opened, then everyone's spirit is heightened,
> Finding within the poem doubly enjoyable sense.

The contribution this little study hopes to make came about by a happy accident. In a seminar devoted to an interpretation of Goethe's philosophical poems, we reached the time when the cooperative interpretations had been concluded and the students were in the final stages of readying their individual papers for presentation. I therefore suggested as a bit of diversion during the intervening two meetings that I try comparable approaches and methods in an attempt to solve the unsolved quatrains of the "Bakis." All I expected from the students was that they keep the chief commentaries before them and check what each had to contribute to the particular quatrain being discussed. I had consulted only Viehoff, and being greatly pressed for time just then, I did what I had so often done with a difficult modern poem: read straight through it several times, without stopping for any obscure or incomprehensible passage. It was this casual approach and unintended "method" of looking at the total configuration before analyzing the individual parts that led to the first broader understanding during the course of the second and third rapid readings. Much was quite plain on the first reading; this in turn made clear still more on further readings, and soon the whole of it was making integrated good sense, except for several obscure passages that still left me perplexed. Just before the first meeting, the pattern of one of the worst, Number 9, first took shape, but it was actually during the meeting that the whole work began to make sense, amid quite a bit of hilarity as one obscure piece after the other would suddenly appear plain and simple—yet with point and grace. I feel sure that the lighthearted and unpurposeful approach contributed not a little to the success. The answer to Number 22, for instance, is so simple and obvious, when one has it, that it is doubly funny for having defied solution so long. By the end of the second meeting, before we had to turn to more serious matters, all but two quatrains and scattered phrases in others had been solved. These have yielded also, I hope, during the time that has since elapsed.

More important than the individual solutions, however, was the discovery of the meaning of the whole, the probable purpose and intent of Goethe in writing these soothsayings. Furthermore, it became obvious that his way of expression and conveyance of meaning here were often the same that he used in his serious poems, and there was thus an unexpected by-product of further insight into his poetic habits of mind and composition. Once the solutions were found, it was clear that the quatrains amount to an informal, aphoristic philosophy of history, of human activity. *History* here does not simply mean conventional political history; it includes more largely the phenomena of man's life on this earth, with the ultimate emphasis on man's creativity, in life and in the arts. The aphorisms are done with whimsy and wit but also with a sovereign insight and a broad perspective that leave them as important for our critical times as they were for the critical 1790's. Except on the surface, we still have not learned the lessons in history that they mean to convey, delighting while instructing.

Since history is such a central concern, the factor of time is given its due place of importance. Images of time dominate the initial quatrains, as they do many a later one. Less obviously, there is also a number symbolism flitting playfully through the work. Provided one is not so solemn as to endow these numbers with a Pythagorean abstract divinity and provided one realizes that here, as so often, Goethe is flavoring the whole with a *jocus serius*, it will do no harm to observe that the numerological arrangement reveals certain patterns. In the first place, there are thirty-two quatrains, that is, the thirty-one that complete a monthly cycle plus the one that (in content also) opens up vistas of continuity into infinity. Also at the end of the first " week," at 7, we have the seven open and concealed faces that signify another cycle that in its continuous revolving leads to the end of all. In the " Sundays " of the month—1, 8, 15, 22, 29—some readers may enjoy seeing subordinate begin-nings of smaller cycles. Then there are the ominous eleventh hour and the triumphant high noon of the twelfth. At unlucky " Friday," Number 13, the poet does reach the nadir of his historical pessimism. Number 16 is at mid-point and appropriately dwells on the three faces of time, the mysterious equivalence of past and future. Numbers 10, 20, and 30 may be related by the motifs of attraction and enjoyment. And so one could go on, about the appropriate content of 2 for the first " Monday," the relation of 12 to 24 in the man of power, and no doubt other number symbolisms intended and unin-tended, as the overingenious mind may extract them.

As for the intent of the whole, the critique of life, time, and history, this should have been apparent long ago. (Perhaps it has been privately to many a perceptive reader in Goethe's time and since.) Indeed, it is precisely in the most plain-spoken and straightforward quatrains that the chief themes are announced, even as the basic attitude is in the motto immediately below the title. Let us begin at the beginning and watch Goethe gradually unfold his meaning.

First of all, the title reads " Weissagungen des Bakis," not " Prophe-zeiungen." I took care to translate it as " soothsayings " (truth sayings, wise sayings), which are not only and simply predictions of the future. Then comes the motto (added later, in 1815):

> *Seltsam ist Propheten Lied;*
> *Doppelt seltsam, was geschieht.*
>
> *Strange indeed is prophet's song;*
> *Doubly strange the event ere long.*

Here plainly and at the beginning is one vital point of the whole: the events of history are actually twice as strange as any prophecies that may be made about them. Nostradamus' prophecies (or those of the Bakis recorded in

Herodotus) are not half so mysterious as the events happening all around us, in our time also. If we can shake ourselves out of our dull unquestioning acceptance of history (or our alarmed prostration before it) and take a fresh, fascinated look at it as it is happening, we shall have a renewed sense of mystery, perchance also a new comprehension.

Before we turn to the main text, we should perhaps note that each quatrain is a double elegiac distich. Each of these, then, consists of a dactylic hexameter and a pentameter, so-called. This is a form long since naturalized in German though less familiar in English and possibly offering some difficulties in the reading, particularly in the pentameter with its medial caesura flanked by two stressed syllables. With such ambiguous verses as these, in which every slightest difference in letter or comma could affect the meaning, it is important to examine the text carefully. The standard Weimar edition, recording all the variants in the original manuscripts and early prints, makes it clear that, throughout, the revisions were chiefly stylistic and the few misprints readily discernable. My text is essentially the Weimar text, though with the modernized spelling and punctuation of the current editions. The latter, however, contain a few arbitrary or uninformed changes in punctuation, which I took care to avoid.

The points made in title and motto, the strangeness of prophecy, the even greater strangeness of events, will gradually be developed as we proceed from soothsaying to soothsaying. The first quatrain concentrates on the people without perspective and their attitude toward those with perspective.

THE SOOTHSAYINGS

I.

Wahnsinn ruft man dem Kalchas, und Wahnsinn ruft man Kassandren,
    Eh man nach Ilion zog, wenn man von Ilion kommt.
Wer kann hören das Morgen und Übermorgen? Nicht einer!
    Denn was gestern und ehgestern gesprochen—wer hörts?

Madness, they said to Calchas, and Madness, they said to Cassandra,
    Ere to Ilion they went, when from Ilion they came.
Who can hear the tomorrow and after tomorrow? Not one can,
    For what was yesterday said, earlier too, who will heed it?

It should be noted incidentally that Herodotus reports (VIII, 20) that the Euboeans similarly disregarded a Bakis oracle until it was too late. The important matter to note, however, is that here, as so often in Goethe, we have an expression of the mystery of time, the strange equivalence of past and future to which I have already referred. The negative instance is the perennial obtuseness of men of action toward men (or women) of insight, whose words are not heeded until it is too late. They cannot see the future, even if a prophet announces it to them, simply because they have never learned to see the past. They are the monoptic and the monochronic of this world.

This quatrain is related to another of similar intent, though of a different point of view, which Goethe wrote much later:

Wer nicht von dreitausend Jahren
    Sich weiss Rechenschaft zu geben,
Bleib im Dunkeln unerfahren,
    Mag von Tag zu Tage leben.

He who fails in his accounting
    Of three thousand years of history,
Let him, inept, in darkness mounting,
    Live from day to day in mystery.

With the second quatrain the difficulties begin. All of the varied solutions thus far are unsatisfactory because they miss the subtle interplay of word and meaning, and, therefore, the point.

2.

Lang und schmal ist ein Weg. Sobald du ihn gehest, so wird er
Breiter; aber du ziehst Schlangengewinde dir nach.
Bist du ans Ende gekommen, so werde der schreckliche Knoten
Dir zur Blume, und du gib sie dem Ganzen dahin.

Long and narrow a road. As soon as you walk it, it broadens.
But—a garland of snakes will you have trailing behind.
Once you have reached the end, may then the horrible knotting
Grow to a flower for you that you may give to the whole.

This quatrain begins to reveal its sense and sequence as soon as we notice the double meaning of *Gewinde* in the second line; this word is more generally used in connection with flowers (a garland) than with snakes and thus establishes the relation to the fourth line. Goethe here, as he does elsewhere, gives expression to one of the tragic facts of life, namely that the very act of living involves a man (or a commonwealth) in wrongdoing, inevitably. This becomes all the more painfully apparent as a man's career develops in scope and power. To illustrate this by an extreme, negative example, one might call to mind those Buddhist monks in Tibet who did not venture forth from their cells in the summertime for fear of the crime of destroying the life crawling beneath their feet. This solution in inaction is one hardly valid or generally acceptable to man; he must resolutely face the fact that action means sin and so conduct his life that the active good he does will in the end far outweigh the wrong in which he will necessarily be involved, realizing that with care and awareness he may actually be able to turn his particular wrongs into a general good.

In the end then, the sinuous reptilian train he engenders as his career and power in life broaden can be transmuted into a thing of goodness and beauty for the benefit of all mankind. Goethe's great illustration of this paradox comes in *Faust*, on the hero's last day on earth, when his tragic crime against Philemon and Baucis leads directly to his abjuring all extraordinary power and to his envisioning a great benefit that he can confer upon millions: the establishment of a free people on a free soil, a people among whom he would like to live as an equal.

3.

*Nicht Zukünftiges nur verkündet Bakis; auch jetzt noch
  Still Verborgenes zeigt er, als ein Kundiger, an.
Wünschelruten sind hier, sie zeigen am Stamm nicht die Schätze;
  Nur in der fühlenden Hand regt sich das magische Reis.*

*Not the future alone does Bakis proclaim; what's at present
  Quietly hidden he too, as a discerner, shows forth.
Rods for divining are here; on the stem they don't show the treasure.
  Only in sentient hand pulsates the magical wand.*

History requires interpretation. The unfolding of the mysteries of place and of times past is fully as much a divinatory act as is the forecasting of the future. The facts of history alone are like the branches on the stem before they are cut and made into divining rods: they are utterly impartial and uninformative. Only after they come into the control of the perceptive searcher do they pulsate with meaning, do they reveal the treasures of their hidden intent. Searcher, rod, and treasure—all these are united in sympathetic vibration.

With the fourth quatrain we face our second deeply obscure, highly metaphorical pronouncement. But here, too, the poet uses figures and images that he has used elsewhere in clearer context, and the meaning is not so inaccessible as it at first seems.

4.

Wenn sich der Hals des Schwanes verkürzt und, mit Menschengesichte,
Sich der prophetische Gast über den Spiegel bestrebt,
Lässt den silbernen Schleier die Schöne dem Nachen entfallen,
Ziehen dem schwimmenden gleich goldene Ströme sich nach.

If the neck of the swan contracts and, with countenance human,
Guest prophetic is bent over the mirror in search,
Then the beauty will let the silver veil fall from the vessel,
After the floating one will golden streams follow at once.

Let us take care not to respond too easily to the romantic stimulus of the word *swan*, taking wing into the distant blue of prophetic swans, swan songs, swan maidens, or Lohengrins. After all, a swan with shortened neck might well be a goose, and Goethe might be having his little joke at the expense of the enthusiast by transforming the exalted into the utilitarian.

He is not, as it happens. Nevertheless, we should do better to begin with the imagery of the whole: it is the imagery of water flowing and reflecting. In this context the strange phenomenon of the shortening of the swan's neck is simply a matter of foreshortening, in the reflected image. If the neck is foreshortened, the head is also, and straight on we see a human face, that of the prophetic guest bent over the mirror. Prophetic swans belong to the past. In the foreshortening of time perspectives, they have become the more humanly striving students of history.

That leaves only the beauty with her silver veil that she lets slip from the boat into the stream. Fortunately for us, the poet names her, does so in the dedicatory poem, "Zueignung," which stands at the head of his collected poems. There it is called "the veil of poetry from the hand of truth" ("Der Dichtung Schleier aus der Hand der Wahrheit"). With the pieces in hand, let us see now whether we can make integral good sense out of the whole.

If the fabled vaticinatory oracle is reduced to the humanly observant guest of time bent over the magic mirror of history, striving to observe its outlines and lines of motion, then truth will allow the poetic, interpretative faculty to come to him on the stream of time. The poetic, creative imagination, far from being an illusory, obscuring curtain between man and truth, is actually the transparent veil coming directly from the hand of truth. It is the medium through which history comes to life and motion for man. Floating down the stream of time, it draws the golden course of history after itself. Vision, study, insight will gain access to the truth, enabling the creative imagination to master the mystery of time.

Here we have learned something that will help us through the other quatrains, obscure and semi-obscure. Each quatrain is a unified whole; the apparent discrepancies are only divergencies in metaphor. Thus, if we truly understand one part, it will serve as a reliable clue to the understanding of the other parts.

5.

Zweie seh ich! den Grossen! ich seh den Grössern! Die beiden
    Reiben, mit feindlicher Kraft, einer den andern sich auf.
Hier ist Felsen und Land, und dort sind Felsen und Wellen!
    Welcher der Grössere sei, redet die Parze nur aus.

Two I see: the great one, I see the greater. The two will
    Grind each other to bits, fierce in belligerent might.
Here there is rock and the mainland, and there there are rocks
        and the billows.
    Which the greater one is, only the Parca will tell.

This is the first quatrain that can be interpreted topically, and it has been so interpreted as referring to continental Napoleonic France in its critical struggle with maritime England—with the end not yet in sight in 1798. This is, of course, correct so far as it goes, but if we rest content with that, we should miss the real point, a point the poet has already made in the preceding quatrains. The deadly struggles of the Napoleonic era are just one example of what keeps on recurring in history. These verses equally well delineate the mortal conflict between the massive land power of Persia and the rocky sea-girt naval power of ancient Greece, with the outcome several times precariously in the balance. And they will equally well illustrate the deadly struggles of our own century. This really is the point Goethe wants to make: he shows us the three faces of time, the mysterious equivalence of past, present, and future, together with the great polarities persisting throughout them, and the Fate brooding over all.

6.

Kommt ein wandernder Fürst, auf kalter Schwelle zu schlafen,
    Schlinge Ceres den Kranz, stille verflechtend, um ihn;
Dann verstummen die Hunde; es wird ein Geier ihn wecken,
    Und ein tätiges Volk freut sich des neuen Geschicks.

May, when a wandering prince lies down on the wintery threshold,
    Ceres fashion her wreath quietly circling his sleep.
Then the dogs will lapse into silence, an eagle will wake him,
    And a vigorous folk joyously greet its new fate.

This quatrain also has been interpreted topically, no doubt with as much particular justice and as much general misapprehension as the preceding one. The specific historical event probably here referred to is not a contemporaneous one, but one from the past that happened to be well known to the times through Kotzebue's dramatic success, the *Gustavus Vasa*, which had its predecessors in the dramas by King Gustavus III and Henry Brooke. The hero of the play is the sixteenth-century founder of the great Swedish dynasty which came to an end later in the Napoleonic era. How he escaped from captivity in Denmark, made his way back to Sweden, was hounded by the victorious Danes with a price on his head, found his first support among the sturdy yeomen of the dales, and turned from pursued to pursuer when the eagle of war (here, as in the "Harzreise im Winter," "Geier" means "eagle"), of resistence against the Danish conquest, aroused him, how he was then crowned king of Sweden (the embattled farmers, the devotees of Ceres, brought him his crown) and led his nation to a new era of power and prosperity—all this can easily be read elsewhere.

The historic point that Goethe apparently wants to make is that of the strange inexplicable catalysis of history in which an able leader, though impoverished and fugitive, offers a point of focus to a defeated, demoralized nation: all suddenly comes to life and integration, leads on to victory and stability. The gray morning hour on the cold threshold turns into the dawn of a new day, the awakening to a new freedom. Something similar happened with Joan of Arc and prostrate France, also with William of Orange, with Washington at Valley Forge, legendarily with William Tell. Goethe perhaps was conjuring up this figure and these events from the past as an image of hope for his own disintegrated, demoralized time, with the wish that it, too, might be only the chilly morning hour, the darkest before dawn.

7.

Sieben gehn verhüllt, und sieben mit offnem Gesichte.
Jene fürchtet das Volk, fürchten die Grossen der Welt.
Aber die andern sinds, die Verräter! von keinem erforschet;
Denn ihr eigen Gesicht birget als Maske den Schalk.

Seven walk enveloped, and seven showing their faces.
Feared are the first by the folk, feared by the great of the world.
Yet the second, indeed, are the traitors, discovered by no one,
For their own face, as mask, hides the rascal within.

To begin with, I should like, just this one time, to offer an interpretation that is probably wrong, however convincing it may be at first sight. It is a traditional one that I initially accepted but more and more felt to be inadequate, for reasons that will become apparent when we turn to the better solution. It may serve as an example of so many interpretations that seem to fit, until we examine the text more closely and exactly.

With all the magic divinatory equipment so proper to the soothsaying of a Bakis, Goethe cannot resist the magic of numbers when he comes to the seventh quatrain, and so he has two different groups of seven conspirators enter upon the stage of history. With the fine irony that always accompanies history, the one group uses obviously conspiratorial means of concealing and masking its purposes, thus drawing both popular and official attention to itself and defeating its own intention of remaining hidden. The successful traitors are those who take no steps to conceal their activities; their open, candid countenances are sufficient mask for their rascality. As always, topical illustrations for this insight could be found in past and present. In Goethe's own day the revolutionary conspirators in Germany, specifically the secret order of the Illuminati, so readily exposed, could be contrasted with such a "candid" character as Talleyrand. From the past there would be the melodrama of Catiline's conspiracy (a secret that was common gossip) versus the open public actions of the two triumvirates. In our own day there have been the cloak-and-dagger conspirators and also the honored expert adviser at the elbow of the man of state.

We cannot, however, rest content with this explication; though it corresponds very well to certain features of the quatrain, it does not agree at all with others, which have simply been pushed aside, explained away. Specifically, we should not find it easy to believe that the poet would introduce two groups of seven conspirators, with the number simply an empty meaningless whim at this point. Thus, another traditional explication, never adequately developed, can serve as our point of departure.

Goethe here means the seven nights and the seven days, the days being a greater secret than the obviously secret nights. These days and nights of the week are indeed the archconspirators against man and all the works of man in their remorseless paired procession through the years, dragging both populace and ruler to the grave and, in the end, also their commonwealth, however mighty. The night, with its bringing of sleep, the brother of death, is the more feared, the more obvious symbol of the final night after the last day. But actually it is the day, the symbol of life and light, with its ceaseless activity, which wears man out and inexorably carries him on to the last day of the last week. The frank open face of rascally day is itself the mask of death.

8.

Gestern war es noch nicht, und weder heute noch morgen
  Wird es, und jeder verspricht Nachbarn und Freunden es schon;
Ja, er verspricht es den Feinden. So edel gehn wir ins neue
  Säklum hinüber, und leer bleibet die Hand und der Mund.

Yesterday it was not there, nor will be today or tomorrow.
  Everyone nevertheless vows it to neighbors and friends,
Vows it even to foes. So nobly then we go striding
  Into the century new—empty our hands and our mouths.

Ironic reflections are these on the starry-eyed attempt of the revolutionary idealists to establish liberty, equality, fraternity by legislative fiat. By proclaiming very loudly that it was there, they assured themselves that they really had established it in the here and now. Filled with missionary zeal, they were determined to bring liberty even to their enemies, " liberating " internal enemies by means of the guillotine, external enemies by force of military conquest. Thus was engendered the fervor which was just then pouring the armies of French tyranny over the face of Europe.

In our day, also, the impassioned social idealists, in their admiration for the words, tend to overlook the acts and intents of the neotyrannies. They continue to use every trick of mental self-deception to keep on believing that the deeds are somehow unimportant, that the millions who perish in the process are as nothing compared to the glorious goal envisaged for mankind. It is an old insight shared by Goethe that the idealist in power becomes the ruthless tyrant sweeping away all human opposition to the realization of his ideal while disregarding the real needs of the people.

It is a neat little touch that Goethe should place this " promise for the new century " in eighth place, the eighth day being Sunday, holiday, the beginning of a new week.

Number 9 is one of the obscurest, if not the obscurest, of the quatrains, and there is one last word that may not be finally solved. I mean the word *Tola*. I trust, however, that I have caught the meaning of the whole and have correctly interpreted most of the specific details.

9.

Mäuse laufen zusammen auf offnem Markte; der Wandrer
  Kommt, auf hölzernem Fuss, vierfach und klappernd heran.
Fliegen die Tauben der Saat in gleichem Momente vorüber:
  Dann ist, Tola, das Glück unter der Erde dir hold.

Mice assemble upon the open market. The wand'rer
  Comes on his wooden foot, fourfold and clattering along.
If the pigeons pass over the seed field at that very moment,
  Then, O Tola, your luck under the earth is assured.

All past attempts at interpretation have been frustrated by two fixed ideas: that the " luck under the earth " can only refer to treasure-trove and that the wooden foot, fourfold and clattering, had to be either a wanderer on crutches or a four-wheeled vehicle.

Let us instead begin by trying to find some common ground among these strange events. It is a bit odd to find the mice assembled on the market place. Just as odd is the conditional that follows: the pigeons flying past the newly seeded field. Normally the former should be in the granaries and the latter would alight on the fields, exacting their toll of the stored and planted grain. Here is the common denominator, the basic image running through the whole: grain, which is, of course, also the fortune from under the earth, under the protection of the goddess Ceres. The mice and the pigeons, therefore, represent the destructive forces, the plunderers; the field of planted cereal represents a constructive force. If line two is parallel to four, with both lines in contrast to lines one and three, the wanderer on wooden foot, moving fourfold and clattering, also represents a constructive force. The only such that can be connected with the grain would be the windmill, not the familiar Dutch type of windmill, but the less familiar kind pivoted on its wooden stilts or supporting base, with its four wings wandering ceaselessly and rattlingly around, grinding the grain into flour for bread.

Thus, we might generalize, if the destructive, parasitic forces of a commonwealth can be diverted from their normal activity, the constructive, creative forces can proceed unimpeded to bring happiness and prosperity to the land. But Goethe neither here nor elsewhere in his reflections on history was a sanguine optimist. Accordingly he states here unreal conditions; he knows full well that the parasitic elements will normally remain quite busy at their depredations and that it would take a certain amount of very clever management on the part of the useful, conserving elements to divert them even temporarily from their nefarious activities, to make the mice (e. g., the local politicians) come out into the open market place or to make the pigeons fly past instead of alighting (on the graft available in every worthy project).

But who or what is Tola? It cannot be an anagram on " O Tal," since Goethe would still have spelled it " Thal." My reference above to " exacting their toll " might suggest a punning relation to *toll* (Zoll). Earlier attempts at explication are even more improbable. More likely and more sensible than any other proposal hitherto is the assumption that *Tola* is the proper name it is presented as being, the name of the place where all these good results may hypothetically come to pass. Tola or Tula is a place name widely disseminated over the world: like its neighbor Thule, it has an aura of remoteness and fabulousness about it. In the legends of origin of various peoples, Tola or Tula is given as the name of the far-distant place whence the people originally migrated. If this interpretation is correct, we are dealing here with a legendary never-never land of the Golden Age, a utopia (nowhere extant), where the parasitic despoiling forces have ceased to impair the work of the creative, constructive elements.

If the reader is vaguely uneasy or strongly dissatisfied with this explanation, he may like to exercise his ingenuity by taking the Hebraic meaning of *Tola* as his point of departure and fitting the rest of the soothsaying around it. As an obscure place name or an early judge in the Old Testament, it leads us nowhere. But I chanced to notice in a Renaissance religious work that the word *Tola* was used for " the Crucified." On asking my colleague in the field, I learned that as a verb, in its participial form, it can indeed mean "suspended" but that the noun "tola" (of different root) means "worm" and, by derivation, "red," "crimson" (the ancient "purple," because of the derivation of the precious dye from the sea snail, *purpura*). As a by-product, to be sure, this makes clear a triple connotative metaphor in Baroque religious poetry which has been a stumbling block to the critics who have not understood its implications, namely *Purpurwurm* as referring to Christ the Crucified. Just how the Hebraic *tola* can be brought into this soothsaying, however, I cannot see, except for the first step: that the worm can be associated with the " luck under the earth."

IO.

Einsam schmückt sich, zu Hause, mit Gold und Seide die Jungfrau;
Nicht vom Spiegel belehrt, fühlt sie das schickliche Kleid.
Tritt sie hervor, so gleicht sie der Magd; nur Einer von allen
Kennt sie: es zeiget sein Aug ihr das vollendete Bild.

Maiden alone at home, with gold and silken adornment,
Senses the suitable dress, not by her mirror informed.
When she goes out, she resembles the servant. But one of the many
Knows her; his eye reveals image perfected: herself.

Who is this young lady so gorgeously dressed at home and so becomingly, even without benefit of reflected image? And why does she dress plainly as a servant girl when she goes out? And who, then, recognizes her and shows her the first reflection of herself in his eyes? Of the varied answers given in the past, the one that no doubt fits best in the total context is the early one by Viehoff (II, 408), namely freedom. And indeed, as the appendix shows, such images as these are variously associated in Goethe's mind with the figure of freedom. The specific interpretation, however, here as elsewhere leaves much to be desired. In closer conformity to the text we can interpret thus: when alone and in seclusion, freedom can reign supreme; with a deeply ingrained sense of the fitness of things and without need of an audience or reflection, she can adorn herself as the queen she is. With this same sense of fitness, she knows that such attire would not do in public. In public life we must have, as the founding fathers so aptly put it, freedom under law; freedom must appear in the guise of the servant girl. Even in this guise, however, she is recognized by the one among all, by the poet; and in his poetic vision she can see the perfect image of herself, namely that she still truly remains freedom even when in the service of the common good.

I I.

Ja, vom Jupiter rollt ihr, mächtig strömende Fluten,
Über Ufer und Damm, Felder und Gärten mit fort.
Einen seh ich! Er sitzt und harfeniert der Verwüstung;
Aber der reissende Strom nimmt auch die Lieder hinweg.

Yes, ye roll from Jupiter, floodtide mightily streaming,
Over the banks and the dam, fields and gardens engulfed.
One I see sitting and playing his harp to the tide of destruction.
Raging, the flood on its course takes away also his songs.

Jupiter Pluvius, the god of storm and flood, presides over this quatrain.
That which is engulfed is represented by the metaphors of bounds and
limitations: bank, dam, field, garden. In the 1790's the floodtide of revolution was breaking through the confines and sweeping away the garden culture
of eighteenth-century Europe. Normally, such a scene of destruction is repug-
nant to the artist, with his strong tendencies to preserve, cherish, and cultivate
the values of civilization and to add creatively to the treasure of tradition.
A poet serves cosmos, not chaos. And yet, there is, at times, the poet who
revels in destruction and celebrates it in his song. There were several such
during this decade of revolution, though usually, like the great Klopstock,
they turned in horror from the Reign of Terror. Topical political poems cannot outlast the occasion but are swept away as debris in the common oblivion.
The poet of the eleventh hour will not survive the twelfth.

The specific picture of the poet rhapsodizing, celebrating the destruction, forbids the extension of this soothsaying to another matter close to
Goethe's heart and also concerned with poetry and destruction. From these
larger perspectives, not included here, all poets and other artists (not merely
the ephemeral poets of this soothsaying), are the sons of time. The poet
may sing undaunted in the midst of destruction, striving for permanence in
the midst of the perishing. Like all else on earth, however, he will be
engulfed by the remorseless stream of time; his work also will perish, sooner
or later, in the passing of the ages.

Mächtig bist du, gebildet zugleich, und alles verneigt sich,
　　Wenn du mit herrlichem Zug über den Markt dich bewegst.
Endlich ist er vorüber. Da lispelt fragend ein jeder:
　　War denn Gerechtigkeit auch in der Tugenden Zug?

Mighty are you and also refined, all bow to your splendor
　　When with a glorious train over the market you pass.
Now at last it is over. But each one whispers the question:
　　Justice—was she among all the virtues that passed?

The frequent topical interpretation of this as referring to Napoleon is, of course, impossible. Not only was he at the time still in republican uniform, but also a contemporary would hardly think of him as being refined as well as mighty. The kind of pageantry with allegorical virtues here described is characteristic of the Renaissance and Baroque. Just such spectacles and triumphal entries did occur in the Europe of Emperor Charles the Fifth, of King Francis the First, and of their princely contemporaries, continuing into the eighteenth century. Goethe, moreover, was fond of looking through the great volumes of engravings illustrating the splendid princely pageantry of those times. His own much-chastened masques written for the festivities at the Weimar court were the last ones of real importance in the great tradition. The old Roman heroes and their triumphs were no doubt also in his mind.

The meaning and intent of the quatrain is clear: the glamor of a mighty and cultivated man at the high noon of his career, with the whole procession of his virtues and accomplishments trailing after him, is so impressive that all misgivings are temporarily stilled. Hardly has the train passed, however, when questions arise as to how well and justly he has used his magnificent endowments.

13.

Mauern seh ich gestürzt, und Mauern seh ich errichtet,
  Hier Gefangene, dort auch der Gefangenen viel.
Ist vielleicht nur die Welt ein grosser Kerker? und frei ist
  Wohl der Tolle, der sich Ketten zu Kränzen erkiest?

Walls I see that are fallen and walls I see newly erected.
  Here the prisoners, there—many the prisoners too.
Is then the world perchance a prison enormous, and free is
  Only the madman who will chains declare to be wreaths?

Here a mordantly bitter reflection on mankind in its never-ceasing struggle for freedom never attained. The Bastille was demolished, but straight-way the Temple was filled again with the victims of the Reign of Terror. Czarist Siberia became Soviet Siberia. Hitler's concentration camp was a local model of the East German total concentration camp, and so on. Hardly has one tyranny been crushed when another arises and man remains prisoner as before. Only the madman, by a process of wild relabeling, can manage to call his bondage freedom.

With Number 13, as is proper, we reach the low point of Goethe's historical reflections.

14.

Lass mich ruhen, ich schlafe. — "Ich aber wache." — Mit nichten! —
*   "Träumst du?" — Ich werde geliebt! — "Frieilich, du redest im*
*   Traum." —*
Wachender, sage, was hast du? — "Da sieh nur alle die Schätze!" —
*   Sehen soll ich? Ein Schatz, wird er mit Augen gesehn?*

Let me rest, I am sleeping. — "But I am awake." — No, you are not. —
*   "Are you dreaming?" — I'm loved. — "Truly you speak in a*
*   dream." —*
Waker, tell me, what ails you? — "Behold the extent of my treasure." —
*   Treasure I am to behold? Can it be seen with the eyes?*

This is the eternal dispute between the dreamer and the man of action, each convinced that he is possessed of the true reality and that the other is living in a world of illusion. This is the accepted and evident solution, but again the interpretations based on it are far less self-evident. One and all interpret this terse dialogue as rendering a verdict in favor of the dreamer and the validity of his world of ideality-reality over against that of the waker. Goethe was hardly so one-sided a thinker; throughout his life his words and actions show that he was well aware of the validity of both sides of the dispute, that it cannot be settled as simple-mindedly as the Platonic idealists would like to believe. Further words of his on the subject, collected in the appendix, make this abundantly clear.

Thus, what he is doing here is showing the human dilemma impartially and objectively. On the one hand, either side can be shown to be living in a world of illusion; on the other hand, each has hold of a reality that is deeply convincing and satisfying to him. The dreamer wants to remain undisturbed. The waker rejoices in his feeling of alertness. To the dreamer, that is an illusion, just as his own conviction of being loved is merely an idle dream to the waker, and the latter's busily accumulated treasure is dismissed as an illusion because real treasure cannot be seen with the eye.

Implicit in all of this is a double critique of history. What is history? Is it the record of the outward course of events and achievements or insight into the dreams and hopes, the artistic and intellectual structures of man? Each individual likewise is in conflict within himself: in school and church he is trained to give his verdict in favor of the dreamer and in principle or theory continues to do so through life, as all the Goethe commentators have done. In the life of activity, daily duty, and personal fulfillment, he soon learns that he can act on those convictions only at his own peril, and he usually proceeds to act on entirely different basic assumptions from those he publicly acknowledges—all this with the well-known tragic psychological outcome, which is only made worse if he quite abandons idealistic motives and attitudes.

15.

Schlüssel liegen im Buche zerstreut, das Rätsel zu lösen,
Denn der prophetische Geist ruft den Verständigen an.
Jene nenn ich die Klügsten, die leicht sich vom Tage belehren
Lassen: es bringt wohl der Tag Rätsel und Lösung zugleich.

Keys are scattered about in the book for solving the riddle,
Since the prophetical mind calls the discerning to see.
Cleverest are those who allow each day to instruct them,
Truly each day will present riddle and answer at once.

The poet offers advice for solving his riddles, and this advice we have
been following. Since the keys lie scattered about in the book, one has to
approach the solution of each part from a knowledge of the whole, that is,
after a repeated traversing of the whole, and after picking up keys whenever
and wherever they appear. The skeleton key probably is a general knowledge
of Goethe's basic assumptions, attitudes, and images.

Still, a discerning mind alone, however acute, will not suffice to solve
these riddles; otherwise, certainly, they would have been solved long ago. As
Goethe suggests, it also takes a certain light-mindedness and spirit of fun,
never worrying and gnawing away at the enigmas, only giving them the minimum of conscious attention, then letting them slip comfortably into the sub-
conscious to simmer away until some day, most favorably in the stimulating
company of others, they will suddenly emerge again accompanied by their own
answers. One can probably never force the solutions (I never had the time
to try); they all come of themselves, like Goethe's favorite mental children and
say, " Da sind wir."

One may indeed imagine that the series of Bakis' soothsayings has
several times in the past hundred and sixty odd years been largely solved in
convivial company amid laughter and pleasant mental stimulation, and in each
case it happened that there just was nobody present to record the feat.

Naturally, these verses also go beyond the merely present. Goethe is
not simply giving directions for reading these soothsayings; he is telling us how
best to read the riddles of life and history. The over-serious, the merely serious
never do succeed in reading them, nor do the ones who persistently keep

31

butting away at one point, insisting on making the breakthrough just there and nowhere else. The keys are simply scattered about, sometimes in the most unlikely places, and a general knowledge of the whole wide terrain is essential to the specialist in any one part of it. The history of science is full of stories of the searchers who came to defeat in an intensive frontal attack on a problem, and sometimes much later, when they were least expecting it, often in the midst of play or conviviality, there would come the solution, all by itself, freely offered—not that such a solution could possibly come to anyone who is not prepared for it.

The last line contains profound wisdom as well as a wry jest: in life, in history, a riddle is often accompanied by its own solution, the only problem then being to find it.

16.

Auch Vergangenes zeigt euch Bakis; denn selbst das Vergangne
    Ruht, verblendete Welt, oft als ein Rätsel vor dir
Wer das Vergangene kennte, der wüsste das Künftige: beides
    Schliesst an heute sich rein als ein Vollendetes an.

Bakis reveals to you also the past, for even the bygone
    Stays, O blinded world, oft as a riddle to you.
He who knows the past, knows also the future, for both will
    Join the today without break as a perfection complete.

Here we have the definition of *soothsaying* that we have been using from the beginning. The prophet with hindsight, the foreshortened prophetic swan, the historian, plays a necessary role in our world; without him we should not know what has happened to us. That dear lady of the anecdote was not so fatuous as she may appear when she said, " How can I know what I think until I hear what I say? " Though the historian may seem to have an easier profession than does the prophet with foresight, that is only so in seeming because of the numbers of the untrained and incompetent attempting to write history. Most of the prophets of foresight, to be sure, are equally incompetent.

The main point comes in the last two lines: genuine hindsight will lead inevitably to genuine foresight—this because of the strange equivalence and mergence of the three parts of time, to which the poet repeatedly alludes in these soothsayings and elsewhere. The three parts together form a perfect single whole. That is why the two types of prophet are often found in one person, as in the Bakis, or in Goethe. Number 16, at the half-way point, is the proper place for such reflections reaching equally backward and forward.

17.

Tun die Himmel sich auf und regnen, so träufelt das Wasser
    Über Felsen und Gras, Mauern und Bäume zugleich.
Kehret die Sonne zurück, so verdampfet vom Steine die Wohltat:
    Nur das Lebendige hält Gabe der Göttlichen fest.

When the heavens open and rain, the water will trickle
    Over the rocks and the grass, over the walls and the trees.
Then, when the sun returns, the blessing steams up from the boulder,
    Only the living holds fast onto the gifts of the gods.

This is a kind of supplement and sequel to the old biblical observation that the rain falls upon the just and the unjust alike—here, rather, it falls impartially upon all. On the other hand, when the sun returns, we see that all do not benefit equally. For the hard and sterile, the benefits soon evaporate without effect; only to the living and fruitful are they a blessing. This is a moral statement, but it is also a historical statement and criticism. If we merely speak of history in terms of the forces that surge through it, we shall fail to understand. The very same forces can have different effects upon various individuals or groups. The same force can bring strength to one, destruction to another, and leave a third unaffected. A boy growing up in the slums amid grinding poverty can become a criminal or a saint, a tramp or a hero, just another slum-dweller or a respectable citizen or a man of wealth. What Goethe says here is, as the biblical allusion indicates, simply a continuation of the wisdom and insight of the ages.

18.

Sag, was zählst du? — " Ich zähle, damit ich die Zehne begreife,
Dann ein andres Zehn, Hundert und Tausend hernach." —
Näher kommst du dazu, sobald du mir folgest. — " Und wie denn? " —
Sage zur Zehne: sei zehn! Dann sind die Tausende dein.

Tell me, what are you counting? — " I count to determine what ten is,
Then another such ten, hundred and thousand thereon." —
Closer to it you will come if you follow my method. — " And how then? " –
Just tell ten to be ten! Then will the thousands be yours.

This is the first of a pair of soothsayings concerned with the problem of number and measurement in historic time and place, yet not just that or even primarily that. The counting man who is being questioned represents the anxious and timid mind among the historians (and other scholars) who is bogged down in the preliminary details, in theories, definitions, formalisms, to such a degree that he never goes on to the important issues. Even more, he does not realize that these preliminary theoretical matters which he is so anxious to settle first are not absolutes, but only matters of arbitrary convention and usage—just like the particular name that is attached to a number, or a rose. Instead of picking away eternally at the Gordian knot, what he had better do is to cut it: in other words, he need simply establish the basic convention according to which he is going to operate (call ten by the name ten; tell ten to be ten); then the larger frame of reference will come all by itself.

In historic periodization, also, so many exceptions, discrepancies, and overlappings can be found that the all too scrupulous person will end with no periods at all. This end result, far from giving the student superior truth and insight into the historical processes, involves him in the chaos of minutiae and keeps him from the attainment of larger perspectives. Such reflections carry us on to the next quatrain.

19.

Hast du die Welle gesehen, die über das Ufer einherschlug?
Siehe die zweite, sie kommt! rollet sich sprühend schon aus!
Gleich erhebt sich die dritte! Fürwahr, du erwartest vergebens,
Dass die letzte sich heut ruhig zu Füssen dir legt.

Did you behold the wave that rolled in over the seashore?
Look, the second, it comes, rolls in foam to its end.
Straightway the third arises. Forsooth, all vain your expectance
That the last may today quietly lie at your feet.

Here, on the one hand, is the problem of historic periodization in the eternal flux of time and events and, on the other hand and more directly, the hopeless outlook for the historian who wants to wait until a historic movement is neatly concluded and rounded off before he proceeds to make his record of it. If he is writing contemporary history, he must learn to interpret events in the midst of results continuing to come in; if he is writing about one period in the past, he must learn to write about it despite the difficulty incurred by the fact that all previous periods led up to it and its aftereffects reverberate into the present. The comic example of disregard of this precept is the German professor of anecdote whose lecture course on the Protestant Reformation started with the first century and had reached only mid-fifteenth by the end of the year.

20.

Einem möcht ich gefallen! so denkt das Mädchen; den Zweiten
Find ich edel und gut, aber er reizet mich nicht.
Wäre der Dritte gewiss, so wäre mir dieser der Liebste.
Ach, dass der Unbestand immer das Lieblichste bleibt!

One I should like to please, so thinks the maiden. The second
Noble and good I esteem, he though is lacking in charm.
If but the third were more certain, I'd surely think him the dearest.
Ah, that inconstancy seems ever the sweetest to us.

In the passing show of life, the gift of attraction and charm belongs to the ephemeral, the billowing cloud, the fragrant flower. Yet for all their glamor one could hardly build a life upon them. On the other hand, the steady and reliable are so unglamorous. Thus far there is common agreement in the interpretation, but that takes care of only gentlemen three and two. Who is number one, to whom the girl would like to be attractive? On this the commentaries are silent and unseeing, yet only with all three do we have the complete cycle and, therewith, the ironic point. Two and three, between whom she can choose, apparently, she does not really want; number one, whom she wants, she cannot choose but can only hope that he may choose her. She will probably have to settle for noble and good number two, giving up hope for number one, who has both glamor and stability, and occasionally sighing for number three, who would have been so exciting.

This matter of commitment to a choice among various possibilities, some of which are mere possibilities, hardly to be realized, is naturally not confined to the young girl during her courting years. She represents the type of private person or historic personage who can spend only a brief and quickly passing time in a state of choice (both happy and painful) and then must commit himself, often settling for much less than he would like, for if he lingers too long, he may end with even less or with nothing. The art is to know when and how to make the commitment, when to stride forth from the dilemma, however attractive the state of choice may be.

21.

Blass erscheinest du mir und tot dem Auge. Wie rufst du
Aus der innern Kraft heiliges Leben empor?
Wär ich dem Auge vollendet, so könntest du ruhig geniessen;
Nur der Mangel erhebt über dich selbst dich hinweg."

Pale you appear to me and dead to the eye. How then do you
Conjure up sanctified life with your indwelling might?
Were I complete to the eye, then you could calmly enjoy me.
Only deficiency will lift you beyond your own self.

This would probably be one of the most baffling enigmas if Viehoff had not over a century ago offered a solution that remains superior to later proposals. Indeed, Goethe's aesthetic writings of these years, in attitude and phrase, confirm his solution. The specific subject of the quatrain is sculpture; symbolized by it are the whole of the arts and, even beyond the arts, the challenge which the imperfect offers to the active, creative, interpretative mind. The marble statue itself is pale and dead to the eye; it does not at all look like a real person; it is in no sense an adequate imitation of life. Yet, with all that, it is vibrant with life and has the power of summoning up a warm living response in the beholder. The poet lets the statue tell the secret of its magic power: if it were perfect and complete, a wholly adequate imitation of a human figure, the beholder would have to put no effort into it, contribute nothing of himself; he could simply relax and enjoy it—or perhaps be depressed by it, as at Mme. Tussaud's.

The very imperfection of the work of art, its incompleteness, serves as a challenge to the beholder to complete it. He himself must become creative when he is confronted by it; thus, in this process of demand and response, he rises to levels beyond himself. The same can be said of other fields of human activity, of the challenge of everyday life, of the challenge of the historic moment.

22.

Zweimal färbt sich das Haar: zuerst aus dem Blonden ins Braune,
  Bis das Braune sodann silbergediegen sich zeigt.
Halb errate das Rätsel! so ist die andere Hälfte
  Völlig dir zu Gebot, dass du die erste bezwingst.

Twice will the hair change color, at first from blond into chestnut,
  Till the brown thereupon silver in value appears.
Solve only half of the riddle, the other will easily follow
  Wholly at your command, that you may conquer the first.

Oddly enough, this riddle has not previously been solved, though once
solved it appears very simple indeed. It depends upon a German pun that
turns out to be no mere pun but something of symbolic import. The first
two lines have always been understood. Goethe begins by stating plainly
enough what happens to the normal European with medium brown hair
coloring. As a child he is usually blond, often a very light blond; as he matures
his hair darkens, often considerably; and then as middle age comes upon him,
it becomes threaded with silver and then quite silvery.

Guessing half of the riddle means merely naming the last stage:
"Weiss," "white," and this, as he promises, will at once suggest the other half
and then the whole: "Weisheit," "wisdom." Indeed, the second half of the
word *silbergediegen* already points in that direction. And to be sure, if a man
has grown old to some good purpose, he will have acquired the "Weisheit"
which will conquer the "weiss." What he acquires inside his head through
the years will more than compensate for what he loses on top of his head.

Here, too, of course, we have the mystery of time, with the cycle suggested from light to dark to light again—all of this not without symbolic intent.

As in the preceding two soothsayings, the active powers of man—his
own control, activity, decision, choice, and commitment—are stressed, not his
helpless victimization by fate and the forces of history. Here specifically man
scores a victory over the remorseless cycle of time by gaining something more
precious than it is able to take from him.

23.

Was erschrickst du? — " Hinweg, hinweg mit diesen Gespenstern!
Zeige die Blume mir doch; zeig mir ein Menschengesicht!
Ja, nun seh ich die Blumen; ich sehe die Menschengesichter." —
Aber ich sehe dich nun selbst als betrognes Gespenst.

Why then are you affrighted? — " Away, away with these specters,
Show me the flower instead, show me a personal face.
Yes, now I see the flowers, I see the faces of persons." —
I though see you yourself now as a specter deceived.

The frame of reference in this quatrain is clear, as are meaning and implication for the most part, if we keep in mind Goethe's botanical studies at this time and especially the philosophical poem he had just written, " The Metamorphosis of Plants." In it the poet gently leads the beloved beyond the formidable first barrier of a harsh scientific nomenclature to an insight into the essentials of botany, showing her what science can reveal to the trained observer about the unfolding of life according to all-encompassing law, law just as applicable to the two of them as to the rest of life.

In the quatrain we have a contrary situation: the layman is frightened and repelled by the schemata, the scientific abstractions, which interfere with his view of tangible reality. Then he is relieved to find the ghostly abstractions gone and to see flowers and human faces once more. However, the layman, who cannot advance from the particular to the general, seems to the scientist to be only a self-deceived ghost. The last line underscores the irony of the mere realist who decries all theory and underlying pattern, who rejects all but the phenomena. By the very act of depriving himself of all relation and relevance, he deprives himself of reality and is left a deluded, dissociated specter.

If we extend these reflections to history, we have the parallel case of the layman's delight in the anecdotal aspects: the exciting events, the striking personalities, the wondrous, the amusing, the scandalous, or the inspiring. If he thinks that these are history, however, then he himself is just an errant specter wandering about through a meaningless procession of particulars. The generalizations, the abstractions, the tracing of lawful processes are what make history history. The need for critical, searching, governing intellect in all fields of man's encounter with his environment is what is being stressed here.

24.

Einer rollet daher, es stehen ruhig die Neune:
    Nach vollendetem Lauf liegen die Viere gestreckt.
Helden finden es schön, gewaltsam treffend zu wirken;
    Denn es vermag nur ein Gott, Kegel und Kugel zu sein.

One comes rolling along, the nine are standing there calmly.
    After the end of the course four lie prone on the ground.
Heroes find it so nice to be so mightily striking,
    For it is only a god who can be ninepin and ball.

The imagery itself is clear; meaning, intention, and implications are also clear for the most part, though there is danger of seeing the last line only from one side and not from the other. Here is the conquering hero under the figure of the bowling ball rolling along on its course and overthrowing what stands in the way. The third line makes a neat satiric point by its use of the word *treffend (striking)*, which has a similar double meaning in both languages. Then from this pleasant surface level the fourth line suddenly plunges down into mysterious depths, stating a theme that haunted Goethe all his life. One thinks at once of a parallel statement in the second " Coptic Song " of a few years earlier, in which, with a metaphor from the smithy instead of the bowling alley, it is said that a man in life must be either anvil or hammer. But that is only the lesser half of this line's implications, for his statement is that only a god is able to be both bowling ball and ninepin. Here the limitation of man (even the mightiest cannot be both) is contrasted with the transcendence of the god (who can be both). This should bring to mind not only Goethe's earlier poem " Limits of Mankind " (" Grenzen der Menschheit ") but also perhaps the motto (and theme) of the fourth part of his autobiography: No one contends against a god unless he is himself a god (" nemo contra deum nisi deus ipse "). God acts upon His creation and at the same time is His creation.

Despite Goethe's concern with this theme, the poet clearly does not intend us in the fourth line to lose ourselves in pantheistic depths; the line has a function to perform in the whole. The center of concern, after all, is man, his action and passion in the world. This is the way the world is, whether we like it or not, whether we deem it just or not. In history there will always be the dynamically striking one who moves along proudly in his career, and there will be those who are swept aside as he rolls onward. So it is, and there is no use in wishing or decreeing that it be otherwise. One consolation, however, remains for the ninepins: just after the bowling ball has swept through them (with relatively small score at that), he himself comes to an ignominious end.—Only a god . . .

25.

Wie viel Äpfel verlangst du für diese Blüten? — " Ein Tausend;
Denn der Blüten sind wohl zwanzig der Tausende hier.
Und von zwanzig nur einen, das find ich billig." — Du bist schon
Glücklich, wenn du dereinst Einen von Tausend behältst.

How many apples do you expect from these blossoms? — " One thousand.
For of blossoms, I deem, twenty thousand are here.
Only one out of twenty, I call that modest." — You may be
Lucky if you in the end keep of the thousand but one.

As previously, in Soothsaying 23, we have here botanical imagery used
to make an important point: even as out of the vast number of blossoms only
a few apples come, so it is in history, in the life of mankind, on the general
and on the particular level. Out of the many promising undertakings of men
and nations, only a few come to fruition; out of the hopes and ambitions of
the individual, only a few are realized; out of the millions of children with
brilliant promise, only a few reach greatness. As Goethe observed in the second
book of his autobiography, " If children grew up according to early indications,
we should have nothing but geniuses." The prodigality of blossoming life is
simply a part of the process of nature; we should not expect too much future
fruit from it. But what of it? The blossoms are so beautiful.

26.

Sprich, wie werd ich die Sperlinge los? so sagte der Gärtner:
Und die Raupen dazu, ferner das Käfergeschlecht,
Maulwurf, Erdfloh, Wespe, die Würmer, das Teufelsgezüchte? —
" Lass sie nur alle, so frisst einer den anderen auf."

Tell me how to get rid of the sparrows, inquired the gard'ner,
Caterpillars as well, brood of the beetles besides,
Mole, flea-beetle, and wasp, the worms, the devil's whole offspring. —
" Leave them alone, then each eats the other in turn."

Once more a biological instance, important enough in itself as a remarkable anticipation of the science of ecology, is intended to point to an even
more important and similar phenomenon. Corruption in government, the depredations of human vermin in the affairs of mankind, have always been there
and probably will be with us always (only not in Tola, perhaps). Our best
hope for combatting them is the achievement of an ecological balance within
which they will help to exterminate one another. The general American
principle of checks and balances helps, and more specifically, the two-party
system achieves that desired end reasonably well so long as each party can
summon the power to throw out the rascals of the other. The two periods of
greatest corruption occurred when one party and then the other was too strong
and in power too long.

In the age of Goethe, in the courts of Europe, large and small, there
was the same swarming of vermin that has existed always and everywhere:
the entrenched in power and the intriguers against them, the staid official and
the ambitious young man, the vested interest and the floating adventurer—each
keeping the other in check through a struggle for mutual extermination. Here
the gardener, the responsible head of state, can save himself much useless grief
and futile activity by standing apart from the actual process of extermination
and simply taking care that the ecological balance is maintained. Several times,
indeed, Goethe plainly and directly advised just such a solution.

27.

Klingeln hör ich: es sind die lustigen Schlittengeläute.
Wie sich die Torheit doch selbst in der Kälte noch rührt!
" Klingeln hörst du? Mich deucht, es ist die eigene Kappe,
Die sich am Ofen dir leis um die Ohren bewegt."

Tinkling I hear: it is the merry bells of the sleigh ride.
Cold as the weather may be, folly will still be about. —
" Tinkling you hear? me thinks it is from the cap you are wearing,
Which, as you sit by the stove, lightly moves round your ears."

The ironic and hilarious point is as lightly seen as made. The old man nodding beside the fire hears the ringing of bells; he thinks it is the young making merry out in the cold; but it is his own cap which is equipped with the bells. The extension is also obvious: the critic of history may be more foolish than the events he criticizes; he will certainly be so if he interprets historical phenomena subjectively or from a limited, opinionated point of view. He himself may well be engendering the folly he blames on the world. Thus, it is not only the *laudator temporis acti* who is here the butt of the joke, the man who has stopped and is resentful that the world has not stopped with him. Though he certainly is at the center of the target, he has many younger companions grouped around him: the subjectivist, the idealist, the doctrinaire, the opinionated of every stripe.

28.

Seht den Vogel! er fliegt von einem Baume zum andern,
Nascht mit geschäftigem Pick unter den Früchten umher.
Frag ihn, er plappert auch wohl und wird dir offen versichern,
Dass er der hehren Natur herrliche Tiefen erpickt.

Look at the bird. He flies from one tree on to the other,
Nibbles with diligent bill pecking away at the fruit.
Ask him, and babble he will, no doubt, and frankly assure you:
That he unpecks the depths glorious of nature divine.

Here is another type of the student and critic of history—or of art, music, literature, science, what you will. His chief outward characteristic is his busy moving about, tasting, smelling, pecking away, making a vast sampling of "probes in depth." In the end, perchance, comes the great collected work, the grandiose survey, put together from all the gathered shreds and patches into a colorful crazy quilt.

It is a pity. The great panoramas are necessary and should be made by the most competent. Occasionally they are, though the really able are usually too busy working at their own special problems, or they stand appalled at the difficulty of making such a general survey at all well. The task is usually done, then, by those who do it much less well: the busy, superficial minds, the birdbrains, the babblers, who can talk on any subject with impressive sounds that make a minimum of coherent sense. Old errors and opinions are copied and perpetuated, with a generous addition of new ones. The author-copyists of these "pecked together" books are the men whom the general public knows as "authorities" on the subject.

29.

Eines kenn ich verehrt, ja angebetet zu Fusse;
  Auf die Scheitel gestellt, wird es von jedem verflucht.
Eines kenn ich, und fest bedruckt es zufrieden die Lippe:
  Doch in dem zweiten Moment ist es der Abscheu der Welt.

One thing I know that, upright, is honored, even is worshipped;
  Turned to stand on its head, it is accursed by all.
One thing I know, it firmly bestows the kiss of contentment;
  Yet at a moment's change loathsome it is to the world.

This and the next are the last of the quatrains that have hitherto successfully defied solution. To be sure, there have been some false solutions based on clues out of context, but they are no longer convincing when we know Goethe's method and approach. If we go his way and keep in mind the intent of the whole, this quatrain, too, should soon yield its meaning. Even putting the whole in slightly different but equivalent words, as a question, will bring us within sight of the solution. What is it, then, that is honored and even worshipped when it is right side up, but abhorred by all when it is upside down? Is it this same thing that firmly, contentedly bestows the kiss (of peace or friendship) but in the next moment would be found too repulsive to be allowed such close intimacy?

The answer is the commonwealth, in its two contrasting phases in the ever turning cycle of historic time. Here again, as in the ninth soothsaying, lines one and three go together, as do two and four by way of contrast. When the commonwealth is right side up, "on its feet," stable, it is an object of respect, even of worship to its inhabitants, who owe so much to it and upon whom it bestows the kiss of peace and prosperity. When the commonwealth is upside down, however, "on its head," unstable, then its inhabitants (and its neighbors, also) become the victims of untold miseries and afflictions; the whole world finds it loathsome and roundly curses it.

From the smaller perspectives, the contemporaneous instance for Goethe was, of course, the degeneration and corruption of the French monarchy which led to the catastrophic "upset" of the revolution and to a still further decline into militaristic tyranny. From the larger perspectives of natural law as it operates on this earth, the rise and fall of commonwealths are simply the macroscopic instances of what happens throughout the lives of individuals and communities: after generation and development come degeneration and dissolution; after the rise comes the decline. It is, of course, a mistake to set a *finis* at this point; this is not an end stage but a transition to a new fresh state, a regeneration, a setting of affairs back on their feet again.

30.

Dieses ist es, das Höchste, zu gleicher Zeit das Gemeinste,
Nun das Schönste, sogleich auch das Abscheulichste nun.
Nur im Schlürfen geniesse du das und koste nicht tiefer:
Unter dem reizenden Schaum sinket die Neige zu Grund.

Lo, this is it, the highest, and yet it is also the basest;
It's the most beautiful now, now a horror to all.
Only sipping enjoy it and do not drink of it deeply;
Under enticing froth sink the dregs to the base.

This time Goethe does literally " present riddle and answer at once."
The answer comes in the third line, though as a verb instead of a noun:
geniessen, enjoy, relish. Restful enjoyment of nature, of the great works of
art and the other achievements of mankind indeed represents the highest
human realization, the most exaltedly beautiful attainment within the power
of an individual or a culture. However, when enjoyment shifts from being
the final crown of a difficult achievement to being a purpose and an end in
itself, when it becomes a self-indulgence, it will lead the individual or the
culture inevitably to degeneracy, its art and civilization to vulgarity, and make
its whole rotten structure detestable.

For the wise and watchful, enjoyment is something to be sipped spar-
ingly, for with its glamorous, frothy surface it can lure the taster to drink more
deeply, down and down to the dregs, whose bitter taste will annul all previous
joy. When enjoyment is an end in itself, it becomes the end of a man or a
culture. As Faust said in comment on the all-too-merry monarch whose realm
was in revolt, " Indulgence debases " (" Geniessen macht gemein " [10259]),
and soon thereafter (10272f) he gives what amounts to a paraphrase of the
preceding quatrain on the topsy-turvy commonwealth.

Seen thus, the quatrain parallels and amplifies the preceding one.
Here, too, if the normal order of things is upset, in this case by an end product's
becoming an end in itself, the good becomes evil, the blessed becomes cursed,
the highest becomes basest, the most beautiful becomes most repulsive. The
same would naturally apply to the other great goods of mankind, which come

as the ultimate rewards of hard striving, such as freedom, which unmerited and unearned becomes license and plunges man or nation into crime. The only safeguard for our great goods is their sparing use after meritorious achievement; under any other conditions they become our greatest curses and the instruments of our self-destruction.

3I.

Ein beweglicher Körper erfreut mich, ewig gewendet
Erst nach Norden, und dann ernst nach der Tiefe hinab.
Doch ein andrer gefällt mir nicht so: er gehorchet den Winden,
Und sein ganzes Talent löst sich in Bücklingen auf.

Fond am I of a movable body, ever directed
First to the north and then earnestly down to the depth.
Yet of another I'm not so fond; it defers to the breezes,
All of its talent dissolves into quick curtsies and bows.

Here the answer is clearly under the sign of compass and weathervane, the compass pointing steadily northward until it is used as a lodestone to point to the ore under the earth. The weathervane, however, is as multi-directional as the breezes that blow; it accommodates itself to every situation; it bows and scrapes to the latest dictates of fashion. It is *charakterlos*, without inward purpose or direction.

It is futile to seek for guidance from the shifting winds of history, but there are certain steady compass points that remain constant through it all, certain great and steady personalities who know from whence they have come and whither they are going. These can serve us as guides, can preserve us from the shifting winds, from the shifting sands, from the remorseless cycle of history—steady, directed, masterful, and in control of the treasurers of this earth. One of these personalties in the history of our changeful world is Goethe. The precept he conveys in his life and work could perhaps be phrased in this way: Know which way the wind blows, but take your direction from the stars.

32.

Ewig wird er euch sein der Eine, der sich in Viele
Teilt und, Einer jedoch, ewig der Einzige bleibt.
Findet in Einem die Vielen, empfindet die Vielen wie Einen,
Und ihr habt den Beginn, habet das Ende der Kunst.

Ever will He be to you the One who does into Many
Sunder Himself, and remains: One, the ever unique.
Find in the One the Many, and feel the Many as Oneness,
And the inception you'll have, have the completion of art.

Here is Goethe's conclusion, which he offers after having touched upon these topics:

the endless variety yet constancy of historic processes (1, 32),
their varied relations to man (5, 7, 17),
man's varied relations to them (6, 15, 27),
his freedom and bondage (8, 13),
his dominance and servitude (12, 24),
the mystery of time and the cyclic course (3, 16, 19),
man's tragic involvement in them and creative triumphs over them (2, 22, 29),
the precarious balance of destructive and constructive forces in man and nature
    (9, 11, 25, 26),
man's striving (and pretending) in the arts and sciences (14, 21, 23, 28),
man's contribution of period and meaning to the ceaselessly surging and end-
    lessly mysterious (4, 18),
the establishment of reliable points of reference (31),
and, finally, man's discreet enjoyment of the fruits of his achievements (10, 20),
with the necessity of being wary lest he be cheated by the very process of
    enjoyment carried a bit too far (30).

Following Goethe's thoughts on these many and varied subjects come the great and deep summation and conciliation in this thirty-second quatrain. The source of the whole mysterious process of places and times, figures and events, is the One, the Eternal One. Everything flows forth from Him; He divides Himself into the multitude of phenomena yet does not lose Himself in them. He remains ever the One.

We who are here as human beings on earth, if we fulfill our microcosmic creativity to the full extent of our powers, will best accomplish our calling by modeling our own endeavors on this ultimate insight of the One in the Many in the One. If our understanding reaches the point at which we perceive the many in one and feel the many as one, then we have attained a mastery in that activity which brings man closest to God: creativity in hand and mind and spirit.

Appropriately, this statement comes as the thirty-second, after the whole monthly cycle of the thirty-one is completed under the double aspect of change and constancy. Herewith, suggestively, we are led into a new cycle of a new world month, with the intimation of increasing cycles winding their parabolic course into eternity.

This seems a solemn note on which to end a comic, even a tragi-comic philosophy of history, but is this not one of the classic and acceptable ways in which a comedy may end? We need not become overly solemn and cite the instance of the *Divine Comedy*, which also ends in the empyrean with the vision of the ultimate mystical oneness. We can find our instance on a far more modest level, commensurate with the little entertainment, the *jocus serius*, the open secret, the public mystery which Goethe here has prepared to divert us and therewith induce us to pause and give thought, serious but not solemn, to what are, after all, ultimate questions concerning man's life in this world of place and time.

Did not Shakespeare also, in one of his lightest works, from the mouth of one of his most whimsical and eccentric characters take the measure of man against the environment through which he strides his course? " All the world's a stage," tossed off so lightly by Jacques, in its persiflage of man's career from the cradle to the grave, is, moreover, only one aspect of the play's measurement of man on earth. It is remarkable how many other aspects come out, ever so casually, in the rest of the comedy, and here, too, we are several times taken to the brink and allowed a glance down into the abyss. Yet everything merges in the final conciliatory scene, as we like it:

> *Then is there mirth in heaven,*
> *When earthly things made even*
> *Atone together.*

APPENDIX

In the text, only few and brief parallels from other works of Goethe are cited. For those readers who are interested in observing similar attitudes, associations, and images elsewhere in Goethe, the following informal group of quotations is added, largely from his aphorisms in prose and verse, though also from other works as my memory and my reading recalled them to me. This is only a specimen collection; any reader of Goethe could easily add more, especially for those soothsayings in which favorite observations and attitudes of the poet find expression. The present group, however, will serve its purpose if it shows how much the " Soothsayings of Bakis " are a part of Goethe's habitual trains of thought or of his patterns of phrase, image, and symbol. It is also reassuring to observe that the interpretations we have made of the quatrains are time and again confirmed by Goethe himself and that certain other interpretations long accepted are quite out of the question.

First, however, we should probably take care of a few preliminaries that may prove to be relevant. It is known that Goethe also wrote a further quatrain of a similar kind which he did not include in the soothsayings, probably because it did not fit in with the intent of the whole. For anyone who is acquainted with Horace Walpole's *Castle of Otranto*, the verses require no commentary. The extensions of meaning are also obvious.

Die Burg von Otranto
Fortsetzungs-Weissagung

Sind die Zimmer sämmtlich besetzt der Burg von Otranto,
  Kommt voll innigen Grimms der erste Riesenbesitzer
Stückweis an und verdrängt die neuen falschen Bewohner,
  Wehe den Fliehenden! weh den Bleibenden! Also geschieht es.

We know of Goethe's interest in the Otranto material in late November, 1798; this quatrain, therefore, may have originated about the same time as another quatrain, with definite date, the one on Virgil's grave. At any rate, the two seem to supplement each other in their contrasting reflections on unworthy and worthy tradition. In the Virgil quatrain we see a great tradition come to new life under the loving care of worthy though remote heirs. It is dated " Den 25. November 1798." The title is post-Goethean.

57

Vom Grabe Virgils

Als das heilige Blatt von Maros Grabe getrennt ward,
  Naht es, der Asche getreu, welkend polarischer Nacht;
Aber im Lande bedeckt von Schnee ergrünt es aufs neue,
  Bietet unwelkenden Schmuck traulich den Grazien an.

Goethe's one further reference in verse to the "Bakis" is included below under the twenty-second soothsaying.

Next, and more important, we should see what Goethe himself had to say about the soothsayings, being mindful to read also these statements in the context of the whole and allowing for various times, moods, and circumstances. There is one incertitude: what he wrote to August Wilhelm Schlegel (March 20, 1800) may have been a momentary slip of the pen or memory; from the correspondence as a whole it would seem that the reference is not to the "Bakis" but to the somewhat similar collection of a year earlier, the "Vier Jahreszeiten," in elegiac couplets, in connection with which it would make better sense. I quote it, nevertheless:

Die Weissagungen des Bakis sollten eigentlich zahlreicher sein, damit selbst die Masse verwirrt machte. Aber der gute Humor, der zu solchen Torheiten gehört, ist leider nicht immer bei der Hand.

How differently the mood of the moment could affect Goethe's remarks on the "Bakis" can be seen in statements made to two old friends late in his life. In 1827 Zelter told him how he had had to explain the close Goethe-Schiller collaboration to a young correspondent who had found the same two distichs in the collected works of each poet. Goethe called this youthful pedanticism a stumbling over straws and apparently associated it with a commentary on the "Bakis" that had come to his attention, for he goes on to say (December 4, 1827):

Ebenso quälen sie sich und mich mit den Weissagungen des Bakis, früher mit dem Hexen-Einmaleins und so manchem andern Unsinn, den man dem schlichten Menschenverstande anzueignen gedenkt. Suchten sie doch die psychisch-sittlich-ästhetischen Rätsel, die in meinen Werken mit freigebigen Händen ausgestreut sind, sich anzueignen und sich ihre Lebensrätsel dadurch aufzuklären! Doch viele tun es ja, und wir wollen nicht zürnen, dass es nicht immer und überall geschieht.

Elsewhere he tells of being similarly afflicted with interpretations of "Das Märchen," of 1795. In his mood of the moment he states that it is futile to try to assimilate such "nonsense" as the "Bakis" to plain human understanding. To be sure, there is no simple one-to-one relationship; such incommensurables cannot merely be " translated " from " metaphoric " to " real " expressions with plain meanings. What can be assimilated are the spiritual-ethical-aesthetic riddles so generously scattered through his works, riddles that were directed to the unriddling of life. This positive part of his statement accords, even verbally, with his observations in Soothsaying 15.

He is in a quite different mood when he answers Marianne von Willemer's letter of about mid-January, 1830. She was baffled by the " Weis-sagungen " and the " Personnenrätsel " and asked for at least a hint toward their solution. Goethe in his answer of April 19 goes into no details but does give a more important general answer when he indicates that some-where from the riddles a deep and lasting excellence will always emerge:

Einige Auskunft über die Rätsel, welche in meinen kleinen Gedichten und den grössern Werken vorkommen, liesse sich anmutig von Mund zu Mund, aber nicht wohl schriftlich mitteilen. Soviel jedoch würde sich durchaus ergeben, dass irgendwo ein V o r z ü g l i c h s t e s, sowohl der Innigkeit als der Dauer nach, auf-fallend entgegenträte.

Not only in " Alexis und Dora " but elsewhere also does Goethe tell us the reason, indeed the necessity, for riddling expression. Two further quo-tations will suffice as comment on his remarks to Marianne.

Die Geheimnisse der Lebenspfade darf und kann man nicht offenbaren; es gibt Steine des Anstosses, über die ein jeder Wanderer stolpern muss. Der Poet aber deutet auf die Stelle hin.
Max Hecker edition of the prose aphorisms, no. 617, included in *Wilhelm Meisters Wanderjahre*, " Aus Makariens Archiv "

Ausserdem hat das Geheimnis sehr grosse Vorteile: denn wenn man dem Menschen gleich und immer sagt, worauf alles ankommt, so denkt er, es sei nichts dahinter.
Wilhelm Meisters Wanderjahre, II, 1

Goethe's faithful assistant, Friedrich Wilhelm Riemer, tells us some-thing about origins and intent in his factually valuable *Mittheilungen über Goethe* (Berlin, 1841, II, 528f.). He was not very bright and misunderstood much, but according to his best lights here is the information he imparts:

Goethe hatte dabei, wie er mir sagte, die Absicht auf jeden Tag im Jahre ein solches Distichon zu machen, damit es eine Art von Stechbüchlein, in der Weise der ehemaligen Spruchkästlein, würde, wie man sonst sich der Bibel, des Gesang-buches &c. dazu bediente, aus einem zufällig aufgeschlagenen Vers ein gutes oder schlimmes Omen, Bestätigung oder Abmahnung und dergl. herzunehmen; oder wie die Alten ihren Homer und Virgil bauchten und daraus ihre *sortes Homericas* und *Virgilianas* zu ziehen pflegten.

In seinem Tagebuche werden sie zuerst unter dem 23. März 1798 notiert. Sie unterhielten ihn aber nur einige Zeit. Da nun ihre Abfassung in die Epoche der französischen Revolution fällt, so ist manches auf die Zeitgeschichte anspielende darin, auch ist es nicht unwahrscheinlich, dass ihn des schon im Faust zelebrierten Nostradamus orakelmässige Prophezeihungen zu einem Versuch ännlicher sibyllinischen Rätselsprüche, als einer poetischen Aufgabe, so gut wie Erfindung von Wahnsinn und Träumen für einen Dichter es sein können, varanlassten. Doch ist nicht alles Weissagung und Rätsel, vieles nur rätselhaft ausgedrückte Sentenzen praktischer Welt- und Lebensweisheit.

He goes on to tell how the lost manuscript was found among the Schiller papers in time for publication with the "Vier Jahreszeiten." Now the latter, in distichs, could possibly be used for sortilege as described; not so the "Bakis" quatrains, and it is hard to see how (considering their content also) Goethe could ever have intended them for such a purpose. Riemer's use of the singular *Distichon* is clear evidence of his confusion between the two. In the second paragraph, where he is really talking about the "Bakis," he perceives the topical and aphoristic sections, but goes on to establish a tradition by assuming that what he does not understand is not understandable. In his final paragraph he cites the words to Zelter in confirmation of the assumption "Dass nichts dahinter zu suchen sei, wenigstens das nicht, was man glaubte." He goes on to tell that at the time of the Zelter letter Goethe had heard of a commentary on the "Bakis" and was curious to see it. But Riemer knows no more about this. Goethe's leter to M. C. V. Töpfer, December 28, 1827, would seem to indicate that the commentary was by Wittich, apparently the pseudonym of the painter-poet Karl Nehrlich, though other rumors, all unconfirmed, are passed down about it.

Though Riemer is quite unreliable as to origins and intentions of the soothsayings, we are on more solid ground when we turn to Goethe's own writings and their implications. The first indication, an obvious one, has long been known; the second one, more intrinsic, has always been overlooked. In his diary for January 11, 1798, Goethe writes: "Nach Tische Aristophanes' 'Ritter,' Übersetzung von Wieland." This translation of *The Knights* appeared in the *Attisches Museum* (1797, I, 2). With it appeared Wieland's note on "O grosser Bakis":

Die Athener hatten einen starken Glauben an gewisse angebliche Weissagungen, die der Sibylle, dem Musäos und anderen begeisterten Personen der fabelharten und heroischen Zeit zugeschrieben wurden. . . . In vorzüglichem Kredit standen, wie es scheint, diejenigen, die den Namen eines gewissen Bakis aus Böotien an der Stirne führten, von welchem man glaubte, dass er die Gabe der Weissagung von den Nymphen empfangen, die auf dem Berge Kithäron einen uralten Tempel hatten. Schon Herodot führt einige Orakel dieses Nympholepten an, die auf den medischen Krieg gedeutet wurden. Wahrscheinlich waren einzelne Personen oder Familien zu Athen in Besitz ganzer Sammlungen von solchen diesem Bakis zuge- schriebenen Chresmologien, glaubten daran einen grossen Schatz zu besitzen und liessen sich gelagentlich von den Schlauköpfen betrügen, welche den Schlüssel zu diesen in seltsame, rätselhafte Bilder und Ausdrücke eingehüllten Geheimnissen zu besitzen vorgaben.

More important is the fact that in 1795 Goethe had translated some of the aphorisms of Hippocrates. A few of them clearly went over into the " Bakis " of three years later and, indeed, into its central image and concept (Hecker, Nos. 626f):

Ich aber will zeigen, dass die bekannten Künste der Menschen natürlichen Bege- benheiten gleich sind, die offenbar oder geheim vorgehen.

Von der Art ist die Weissagekunst. Sie erkennet aus dem Offenbaren das Ver- borgene, aus dem Gegenwärtigen das Zukünftige, aus dem Toten das Lebendige und den Sinn des Sinnlosen.

The remaining Bakis references in Goethe are of small importance. More important are general remarks of his on attitude and intent. First cited are two sets of verses on his use of the *jocus serius* (Hecker edition of the verse aphorisms, pp. 14, 41):

Wenn ich den Scherz will ernsthaft nehmen,
So soll mich niemand drum beschämen;
Und wenn ich den Ernst will scherzhaft treiben,
So werd ich immer derselbe bleiben.

Sei das Werte solcher Sendung
Tiefen Sinnes heitre Wendung.

Both earlier and later the poet explained the necessity for indirect expression, for instance through a juxtaposition of images, if his deeper intent were to be conveyed. He wrote to Charlotte von Stein (April 6, 1782):

In allen solchen Kompositionen muss der Verfasser wissen, was er will, aber nirgends dogmatisieren, er muss in tausend versteckten Gestalten (niemals grade zu), andeuten und merken lassen, wo es hinaus soll.

Much later (September 27, 1827) to Carl Jacob Ludwig Iken he wrote:

Da sich gar manches unserer Erfahrungen nicht rund aussprechen und direkt mit- teilen lässt, so habe ich seit langem das Mittel gewählt, durch einander gegenü- bergestellte und sich gleichsam ineinander abspiegelnde Gebilde den geheimeren Sinn dem Aufmerkenden zu offenbaren.

His little essay "Wiederholte Spiegelungen," of 1823, takes up other aspects less relevant here.

Since in the course of our examination of the soothsayings we had occasion time and again to observe how history repeats itself, how the particular falls into the pattern of the general, we should perhaps hear how Goethe formulates the matter (Hecker, Nos. 569 and 571):

Das Allgemeine und Besondere fallen zusammen . . .
. . . deswegen denn auch das Besonderste, das sich ereignet, immer als Bild und Gleichnis des Allgemeinsten auftritt.

In a letter to C. E. Schubarth (April 2, 1818) Goethe wrote:

Alles, was geschieht, ist Symbol, und indem es volkommen sich selbst darstellt, deutet es auf das übrige.

The last of the general parallels may serve to illustrate how close in language and diction and in word and phrase association the soothsayings are to other works of that time, here specifically to what is said about the poet early in *Wilhelm Meisters Lehrjahre* (II, 2). Note how many echoes from even this one sentence of a few years earlier are scattered through the soothsayings, well beyond their concentration in 14 and 16:

So lebt er [der Dichter] den Traum des Lebens als ein Wachender, und das Seltenste, was geschieht, ist ihm zugleich Vergangenheit und Zukunft. Und so ist der Dichter zugleich Lehrer, Wahrsager, Freund der Götter und der Menschen.

From this point onward we can simply list each quotation under the number of the soothsaying to which it is parallel. (Several could be listed under two or more numbers.) After what we have just read from Goethe, it will not come as a surprise that many a quotation will shed further light on a soothsaying by the process of mutual reflection so nicely formulated by the poet. Analogous to the motto and the first quatrain are these observations:

I.

" Du sagst gar wunderliche Dinge! "
Beschaut sie nur, sie sind geringe;
Wird Vers und Reim denn angeklagt,
Wenn Leben und Prosa das Tollste sagt?

Hecker, Verse p. 118

Leider muss man nur meistenteils verstummen, um nicht wie Cassandra, für wahn-
sinnig gehalten zu werden, wenn man das weissagt, was schon vor der Tür ist.

letter to an unknown recipient, before October, 1795,
W. A., Briefe, 18, 71

Ist denn so gross das Geheimniss, was Gott und der Mensch und die
    Welt sei?
Nein! Doch niemand hörts gerne; da bleibt es geheim.

"Epigramme. Venedig, 1790," No. 65

2.

Die Tätigkeit ist, was den Menschen glücklich macht,
Die, erst das Gute schaffend, bald ein Übel selbst
Durch göttlich wirkende Gewalt in Gutes kehrt.

"Paläophron und Neoterpe, Festspiel, 1800"

Schadet ein Irrtum wohl? Nicht immer. Aber das Irren,
    Immer schadets. Wie sehr, sieht man am Ende des Wegs.

"Vier Jahreszeiten," Herbst 50

Irrtum verlässt uns nie; doch ziehet ein höher Bedürfnis
    Immer den strebenden Geist leise zur Wahrheit hinan.

"Vier Jahreszeiten," Herbst, 52

Mit jedem Schritt wird weiter
Die rasch Lebensbahn.

"Bundeslied," last stanza

3.

Was ist das Schwerste von allen? Was dir das Leichteste dünket,
    Mit den Augen zu sehen, was vor den Augen dir liegt.

"Xenien," Nachlass 45

4.

Ehren lehrest du sie [die Söhne] das Vergangene und schätzen
    vor allem
Jeglichen Tages Wert und in dem Neuen die Vorzeit.
. . . .
Der den Augenblick kennt, dem unverschleiert die Zukunft
In der stillen Minute des hohen Denkens erscheint.

"Episteln," 1795–96. Skizzen zur dritten Epistel

Wer in der Weltgeschichte lebt
Dem Augenblick sollt' er sich richten?
Wer in die Zeiten schaut und strebt,
Nur der ist wert, zu sprechen und zu dichten.

Hecker, Verse p. 67

5.

Nur Meer und Erde haben hier Gewicht,
Ist jenem erst das Ufer abgewonnen,
Dass sich daran die stolze Woge bricht,
So tritt durch weisen Schluss, durch Machtgefechte
Das feste Land in alle seine Rechte.

"Ihro der Kaiserin von Frankreich Majestät, 1812"

O, was sind wir Grossen auf der Woge der Menschheit? Wir glauben sie zu beherrschen, und sie treibt uns auf und nieder, hin und her.

Egmont, Act I

Ich sehe Geister vor mir, die still und sinnend auf schwarzen Schalen das Geschick der Fürsten und vieler Tausende wägen. Langsam wankt das Zünglein auf und ab; tief scheinen die Richter zu sinnen; zuletzt sinkt diese Schale, steigt jene, angehaucht vom Eigensinn des Schicksals, und entschieden ists.

Egmont, Act IV

6.

Sei'n wir unbesorgt! Der Herzog gehört zu den Urdämonen, deren granitartiger Charakter sich niemals beugt, und die gleichwohl nicht untergehen können. Er wird stets aus allen Gefahren unversehrt hervorgehen. Das weiss er recht gut selbst, und darum kann er so Vieles wagen und versuchen, was jeden Andern längst zu Grunde gerichtet hätte.

conversation with Friedrich von Müller, *ca.* 1809,
Biedermann II, 106

Der lang ersehnte Friede nahet wieder,
Und alles scheint umkränzet und umlaubt;
Hier legt die Wut die scharfen Waffen nieder,
Dem Sieger ist sogar der Helm geraubt;
Das nahe Glück erreget frohe Lieder
Und Scherz und laute Freude sind erlaubt. . . .

Und Ceres wird versöhnet und verehret,
Die wieder froh die goldnen Ähren regt;
Wenn dann die Fülle prächtig wiederkehret,
Die aller Freuden reiche Kränze trägt. . . .

"Maskenzug. Zum 30. Januar 1798"

7.

Da ich in Jahrtausenden lebe, so kommt es mir immer wunderlich vor, wenn ich von Statuen und Monumenten höre. Ich kann nicht an eine Bildsäule denken, die einem verdienten Mann gesetzt wird, ohne sie im Geiste schon von künftigen Kriegern umgeworfen und zerschlagen zu sehen.

conversation with Eckermann, July 5, 1827

Wie auch die Welt sich stellen mag,
Der Tag immer belügt den Tag.

Hecker, Verse p. 123

8.

Könige wollen das Gute, die Demagogen desgleichen,
Sagt man; doch irren sie sich; Menschen, ach, sind sie, wie wir.

"Epigramme. Venedig, 1790," 51

Er [Geheimrat von S.] hatte die Willkür der Nation, die nur vom Gesetz sprach, kennen gelernt und den Unterdrückungsgeist derer, die das Wort Freiheit immer im Munde führten. Er hatte gesehen, dass auch in diesem Falle der grosse Haufe sich treu blieb und Wort für Tat, Schein für Besitz mit grosser Heftigkeit aufnahm.

Unterhaltungen deutscher Ausgewanderter, 1795, introduction

Als man hörte vom Rechte der Menschen, das allen gemein sei,
Von der begeisternden Freiheit und von der löblichen Gleichheit!
Damals hoffte jeder, sich selbst zu leben. . . .
. . . .
Aber der Himmel trübte sich bald. Um den Vorteil der Herrschaft
Stritt ein verderbtes Geschlecht, unwürdig das Gute zu schaffen.
Sie ermordeten sich und unterdrückten die neuen
Nachbarn und Brüder und sandten die eigennützige Menge.

Hermann und Dorothea, 1797,
Klio, canto six, near beginning

And after the defeat of Napoleon and the Congress of Vienna:

Sie werden so lange votieren und schnacken,
Wir sehen endlich wieder Kosaken;
Die haben uns vom Tyrannen befreit,
Sie befreien uns auch wohl von der Freiheit.

Hecker, Verse p. 167

9.

Aber wissen Sie was? Die Welt soll nicht so rasch zum Ziele als wir denken und wünschen. Immer sind die retardierenden Dämonen da, die überall dazwischen und überall entgegentreten, so dass es zwar im ganzen vorwärts geht, aber sehr langsam. Aber lass die Menschheit dauern so lange sie will, es wird ihr nie an Hindernissen fehlen, die ihr zu schaffen machen, und nie an allerlei Not, damit sie ihre Kräfte entwickele.

conversation with Eckermann, October 23, 1828

10.

Es gibt zwei friedliche Gewalten: das Recht und die Schicklichkeit.

Hecker, No. 543

Freiheit ist ein herrlicher Schmuck, der schönste von allen,
Und doch steht er, wir sehn's, wahrlich nicht jeglichen an.

"Xenien," Nachlass 183

Wie anders trat jene dagegen auf! . . . Herrlich gebildet, in ihrem Wesen und Betragen als eine Tochter der Freiheit anzusehen. Das Gefühl ihrer selbst gab ihr Würde ohne Stolz; ihre Kleider ziemten ihr, sie umhüllten jedes Glied, ohne es zu zwängen, und die reichlichen Falten des Stoffes wiederholten, wie ein tausendfaches Echo, die reizenden Bewegungen der Göottlichen.

Wilhelm Meisters Lehrjahre, I, 8

II

Goethe is commenting on Soulavie's memoires of the reign of Louis XVI:

Im ganzen ist es der ungeheure Anblick von Bächen und Strömen, die sich nach Naturnotwendigkeit von vielen Höhen und aus vielen Tälern gegeneinander stürzen und endlich das Übersteigen eines grossen Flusses und eine Überschwemmung veranlassen, in der zugrunde geht, wer sie vorgesehen hat, so gut als der sie nicht ahndete.

letter to Schiller, March 9, 1802

Sowie ein Dichter politisch wirken will, muss er sich einer Partei hingeben, und sowie er dieses tut, ist er als Poet verloren; er muss seinem freien Geiste, seinem unbefangenen Überblick Lebewohl sagen und dagegen die Kappe der Borniertheit und des blinden Hasses über die Ohren ziehen.

conversation with Eckermann, early 1832,
Biedermann IV, 436

Auch ist ein politisches Gedicht immer nur als Produkt eines gewissen Zeitzustandes anzusehen, der aber freilich vorübergeht und dem Gedicht für die Folge denjenigen Wert nimmt, den es vom Gegenstand hat.

conversation with Eckermann, March 10, 1830

Manches Herrliche der Welt
Ist in Krieg und Streit zerronnen;
Wer beschützet und erhält,
Hat das schönste Los gewonnen.

Hecker, Verse p. 194

12

Sicher tret' ich auf und glanzumgeben;
Jedes Auge freut sich meines Kommens,
Jedes Herz erhebt sich gleich zur Hoffnung,
Jeder Geist, schon schwelget er in Wünschen
Denn die Weisheit, wandelt sie bescheiden . . .
Wenig achtet sie der Haufe. . . .
Aber wenn sie sich zur Macht gesellet,
Neiget gleich sich die erstaunte Menge.

"Vorspiel zu Eröffnung des Weimarischen Theaters
am 19. September 1807." "Die Majestät" is speaking.

Wenn das Publikum von einem Helden hört, der grosse Taten getan hat, so malt es sich ihn gleich, nach der Bequemlichkeit einer allgemeinen Vorstellung, fein hoch und wohlgebildet; eben so pflegt man auch einem Menschen, der sonst viel gewirkt hat, die Reinheit, Klarheit und Richtigkeit des Verstandes zuzuschreiben. Man pflegt, sich ihn ohne Vorurteile, unterrichtet und gerecht zu denken.

letter to Merck, November 14, 1781

13.

So viel kann ich sagen, je grösser die Welt desto garstiger wird die Farce, und ich schwöre, keine Zote und Eselei der Hanswurstiaden ist so ekelhaft als das Wesen der Grossen, Mittlern und Kleinen durcheinander.

letter to Charlotte von Stein, Berlin, May 19, 1778

Und wenn Sie . . . alle Quellen . . . zu durchforschen vermöchten, was würden Sie finden? Nichts anderes ale eine grosse Wahrheit, die längst entdeckt ist . . . , dass es zu allen Zeiten und in allen Ländern miserabel gewesen ist. Die Menschen haben sich stets geängstigt und geplagt, sie haben sich untereinander gequält und gemartert. . . .

conversation with Heinrich Luden, August 19, 1806

> *O weh! hinweg! und lasst mir jene Streite*
> *Von Tyrannei und Sklaverei beiseite.*
> *Mich langeweilt's; denn kaum ist's abgetan,*
> *So fangen sie von vorne wieder an;*
> *Und keiner merkt: es ist doch nur geneckt*
> *Vom Asmodeus, der dahinter steckt.*
> *Sie streiten sich, so heisst's, um Freiheitsrechte;*
> *Genau besehn, sind's Knechte gegen Knechte.*

Mephistopheles in Faust II, Act 2, 6956–63

. . . so bemerken wir: . . . dass Freiheit und Gleichheit nur in dem Taumel des Wahnsinns genossen werden können. . . .

Das Römische Carneval, 1789, conclusion

14.

Zierlich Denken und süss Erinnern
Ist das Leben im tiefsten Innern.

Ich träumt' und liebte sonnenklar;
Dass ich lebte, ward ich gewahr.

Hecker, Verse p. 28

Sarastro: In diesen stillen Mauern lernt der Mensch sich selbst und sein Innerstes erforschen. Er bereitet sich vor, die Stimme der Götter zu vernehmen; aber die erhabene Sprache der Natur, die Töne der bedürftigen Menschheit lernt nur der Wandrer kennen, der auf den weiten Gefilden der Erde umherschweift.

Die Zauberflöte zweiter Teil, 1798

Epimenides: *Doch schäm' ich mich der Ruhestunden,*
Mit euch zu leiden war Gewinn:
Denn für den Schmerz, den ihr empfunden,
Seid ihr auch grösser als ich bin.
Priester: *Tadle nicht der Götter Willen,*
Wenn du manches Jahr gewannst:
Sie bewahrten dich im Stillen,
Dass du rein empfinden kannst.

Des Epimenides Erwachen, 1814, II, 9

Alle Menschen guter Art empfinden bei zunehmender Bildung, dass sie auf der Welt eine doppelte Rolle zu spielen haben, eine wirkliche und eine ideelle, und in diesem Gefühl ist der Grund alles Edlen aufzusuchen. Was uns für eine wirkliche zugeteilt sei, erfahren wir nur allzu deutlich; was die zweite betrifft, darüber können wir selten ins klare kommen. Der Mensch mag seine höhere Bestimmung auf Erden oder im Himmel, in der Gegenwart oder in der Zukunft suchen, so bleibt er deshalb doch innerlich einem ewigen Schwanken, von aussen einer immer störenden Einwirkung ausgesetzt, bis er ein für allemal den Entschluss fasst, zu erklären, das Rechte sei das, was ihm gemäss ist.

Dichtung und Wahrheit, Book 11

15.

Talismane werd' ich in dem Buch zerstreuen,
Das bewirkt ein Gleichgewicht.
Wer mit gläubiger Nadel sticht,
Überall soll gutes Wort ihm freuen.

> West-Östlicher Divan, 1819, Buch der Sprüche, motto

Meyer pflegt immer zu sagen, fiel Goethe lachend ein, wenn nur das Denken nicht so schwer wäre! — Das Schlimme aber ist, fuhr er heiter fort, dass alles Denken zum Denken nichts hilft; man muss von Natur richtig sein, so dass die guten Einfälle immer wie freie Kinder Gottes vor uns dastehen und uns zurufen: da sind wir!

> conversation with Eckermann, February 24, 1824, conclusion

16.

Liegt dir Gestern klar und offen,
Wirkst du heute kräftig frei,
Kannst auch auf ein Morgen hoffen,
Das nicht minder glücklich sei.

> Hecker, Verse p. 104

Breme: . . . das Theatrum Europeum kenn ich in- und auswendig. Wer recht versteht was geschehen ist, der weiss auch, was geschieht und geschehen wird.

> *Die Aufgeregten,* IV, 1

17.

Bilden wohl kann der Verstand, doch der tote kann nicht beseelen,
Aus dem Lebendigen quillt alles Lebendige nur.

> "Votiftafeln," 29, "Verstand"

18.

Ich bin auf Wort, Sprache und Bild im eigentlichsten Sinne angewiesen und völlig unfähig, durch Zeichen und Zahlen . . . auf irgendeine Weise zu operieren.

letter to Carl Friedrich Naumann, January 24, 1826

Es ist mit der Geschichte wie mit der Natur, wie mit allem Profunden, es sei vergangen, gegenwärtig oder zukünftig: je tiefer man ernstlich eindringt, desto schwierigere Probleme tun sich hervor. Wer sie nicht fürchtet, sondern kühn darauf losgeht, fühlt sich, indem er weiter gedeiht, höher gebildet und behaglicher.

Hecker, No. 944

19.

Das Meer flutet immer,
Das Land behält es nimmer.

Hecker, Verse p. 57

Die Zeit aber ist in ewigem Fortschreiten begriffen, und die menschlichen Dinge haben alle fünfzig Jahre eine andere Gestalt, so dass eine Einrichtung, die im Jahre 1800 eine Vollkommenheit war, schon im Jahre 1850 vielleicht ein Gebrechen ist.

conversation with Eckermann, January 4, 1824

Alles ist einem ewigen Wechsel unterworfen, und da gewisse Dinge nicht nebeneinander bestehen können, verdrängen sie einander.

"Einleitung in die Propyläen," 1798

20.

Du verklagest das Weib, sie schwanke von einem zum andern!
Tadle sie nicht: sie sucht einen beständigen Mann.
"Antiker Form sich nähernd," Entschuldigung, 1782

Warum bin ich vergänglich, o Zeus? so fragte die Schönheit.
Macht ich doch, sagte der Gott, nur das Vergängliche schön.
"Vier Jahreszeiten," Sommer 35

21

Doch dieses merke, der Fuss ist von Marmor, er verlangt nicht zu gehen, und so ist der Körper auch, er verlangt nicht zu leben . . . kein echter Künstler verlangt sein Werk neben ein Naturprodukt oder gar an dessen Stelle zu setzen. . . . Hätte Pygmalion seiner Statue begehren können, so wäre er ein Pfuscher gewesen. . . .

"Diderots Versuch über die Malerei,"
Goethe's running commentary and critique, 1798

. . . selten dass ein Künstler sowohl in die Tiefe der Gegenstände, als in die Tiefe seines eignen Gemüts zu dringen vermag, um in seinen Werken . . . wetteifernd mit der Natur, etwas geistig Organisches hervorzubringen und seinem Kunstwerk einen solchen Gehalt, eine solche Form zu geben, wodurch es natürlich zugleich und übernatürlich erscheint.

"Einleitung in die Propyläen," 1798

Ihr kommt Gebildetes allhier zu schauen,
Gebildet scheinbar, doch ein lebend Bild;
So weiss die Kunst vielfältig anzubauen
Der Fabel, der Geschichte reich Gefild. . . .
Und so entgegnen wir euch, starr erscheinend,
Lebendig, uns zu eurer Lust vereinend.

"Bilder-Szenen. Den 15. März 1816
bei Freiherrn von Helldorff"

Kannst du die Bedeutung lesen,
Ihren Sinn verlierst du nie:
Beide sind nur tote Wesen,
Und die Kunst belebte sie.

"Urne auf einem bunten Teppich,"
1826, one of a set of emblems

Da Künstler und Liebhaber, oder vielmehr Künstler und das grosse Publikum sehr oft über Wahrheit und Wahrscheinlichkeit im Widerspruche stehen, indem die Menge nach gewissen Vorstellungsarten das Kunstwerk so wahr als möglich haben, der Künstler aber auf seinem Wege es nicht einmal zur Wahrscheinlichkeit bringen, sondern verlangen kann, dass man sich in seine Welt versetze, so ist diese Frage in einem heitern Gespräche ausgeführt.

"Anzeige der Propyläen," 1798

Zuschauer: Nun sagen Sie mir: warum erscheint auch mir ein vollkommenes Kunstwerk als ein Naturwerk?

Anwalt: Weil es mit Ihrer bessern Natur übereinstimmt, weil es übernatürlich, aber nicht aussernatürlich ist. Ein vollkommenes Kunstwerk ist ein Werk des menschlichen Geistes und in diesem Sinne auch ein Werk der Natur.

"Über Wahrheit und Wahrscheinlichkeit der Kunstwerke. Ein Gespräch," 1798

Es begegnete und geschieht mir noch, dass ein Werk bildender Kunst mir bei'm ersten Anblick missfällt, weil ich ihm nicht gewachsen bin; ahnd' ich aber ein Verdienst daran, so such' ich ihm beizukommen, und dann fehlt es nicht an den erfreulichsten Entdeckungen: an den Dingen werd' ich neue Eigenschaften und an mir neue Fähigkeiten gewahr.

Hecker, No. 162

22.

War doch gestern dein Haupt noch so braun wie die Locke der Lieben,
Deren holdes Gebild still aus der Ferne mir winkt;
Silbergrau bezeichnet dir früh der Schnee nun die Gipfel,
Der sich in stürmender Nacht dir um den Scheitel ergoss.
Jugend, ach! ist dem Alter so nah, durchs Leben verbunden,
Wie ein beweglicher Traum Gestern und Heute verband.

"Schweizeralpe," 1797

Gönnet immer fort und fort
Bakis eure Gnade:
Des Propheten tiefstes Wort
Oft ist's nur Scharade.

Hecker, Verse p. 94

23.

Wer sich vor der Idee scheut, hat auch zuletzt den Begriff nicht mehr.

Hecker, No. 128

Man wird nie betrogen, man betrügt sich selbst.

Hecker, No. 681

Wissenschaften entfernen sich im Ganzen immer vom Leben und kehren nur durch einen Umweg wieder dahin zurück.

Hecker, No. 691

Wärt ihr, Schwärmer, im Stande die Ideale zu fassen,
O so verehrtet ihr auch, wie sichs gebührt, die Natur.
Wärt ihr, Philister, im Stand die Natur im Grossen zu sehen,
Sicher führte sie selbst euch zu Ideen empor.

"Votiftafeln," 4, 1796

Freundinnen, welche mich schon früher den einsamen Gebirgen, der Betrachtung starrer Felsen gern entzogen hätten, waren auch mit meiner abstrakten Gärtnerei keineswegs zufrieden. Pflanzen und Blumen sollten sich durch Gestalt, Farbe, Geruch auszeichnen, nun verschwanden sie aber zu einem gespensterhaften Schemen.

"Die Metamorphose der Pflanzen,"
introduction to the poem

24.

Ich scheine dem Ziele dramatischen Wesens immer näher zu kommen, da michs nun immer näher angeht, wie die Grossen mit den Menschen und die Götter mit den Grossen spielen.

letter to Charlotte von Stein, Wörlitz, May 14, 1778

Der Handelnde ist immer gewissenlos; es hat niemand Gewissen als der Betrachtende.

Hecker, No. 241

Grosse, von Ewigkeit her oder in der Zeit entwickelte, ursprüngliche Kräfte wirken unaufhaltsam, ob nutzend oder schadend, das ist zufällig

Hecker, No. 374

Wer ist denn der souveräne Mann?
Das ist bald gesagt:
Der, den man nicht hindern kann,
Ober er nach Gutem oder Bösem jagt.

Hecker, Verse p. 35

Helden, herrlich zu sein, beschädigen Tausende. Tadelt
Nicht den Dichter, der auch wie ein Eroberer denkt.

"Epigramme. Venedig, 1790," Nachlese 21

25.

Ich aber bete D e n an, der eine solche Produktionskraft in die Welt gelegt hat, dass, wenn auch nur der millionste Teil davon ins Leben tritt, die Welt von Geschöpfen wimmelt.

conversation with Eckermann, February 20, 1831

"Die Natur tut nichts umsonst," ist ein altes Philisterwort. Sie wirkt ewig lebendig, überflüssig und verschwenderisch, damit das Unendliche immerfort gegenwärtig sei, weil nichts verharren kann.

letter to Zelter, August 13, 1831

26.

Du weisst aber, wenn die Blattläuse auf den Rosenzweigen sitzen und sich hübsch dick und grün gesogen haben, dann kommen die Ameisen und saugen ihnen den filtrirten Saft aus den Leibern. Und so gehts weiter.

letter to Knebel, April 17, 1782

Jeder solcher Lumpenhunde
Wird vom zweiten abgetan;
Sei nur brav zu jeder Stunde,
Niemand hat dir etwas an.

Hecker, Verse p. 131

Indem man unverbesserliche Übel an Menschen und Umständen verbessern will, verliert man die Zeit und verdirbt noch mehr, statt dass man diese Mängel annehmen sollte, gleichsam als Grundstoff, und nachher suchen diese zu contrebalancieren.

Tagebuch, December 14, 1778

27.

"Der Mond soll im Kalender stehn;
Doch auf den Strassen ist er nicht zu sehn!
Warum darauf die Polizei nicht achtet?"
Mein Freund, urteile nicht so schnell!
Du tust gewaltig klug und hell,
Wenn es in deinem Kopfe nachtet.

Hecker, Verse p. 133

Lange werden wir euch noch ärgern und werden euch sagen:
Rote Kappen, euch fehlt nur das Glöckchen zum Putz.
"Xenien," 189, "Das Requisit," 1796

28.

Lauter neue Bücher, die er [der Schuhu] nach dem Geruche rezensiert hat! Hier sind die grossen Lexika, die grossen Krambuden der Literatur, wo jeder einzeln sein Bedürfnis pfennigweise nach dem Alphabet abholen kann.
Die Vögel, 1780

Führ uns hin!
Dass wir da trippeln,
Dass wir uns freuen,
Naschen und flattern —
Rühmliche Wonne!
Mandeln zu knuspern!
Erbsen zu schlucken!
Würmchen zu lesen!
Preisliches Glück!
Führ uns hin!

Die Vögel

29.

Es ist kein schönrer Anblick in der Welt,
Als einen Fürsten sehn, der klug regieret,
Das Reich zu sehn, wo jeder stolz gehorcht,
Wo jeder sich nur selbst zu dienen glaubt,
Weil ihm das Rechte nur befohlen wird.
Antonio in *Torquato Tasso*, I, 4

O diese Zeit hat fürchterliche Zeichen,
Das Niedre schwillt, das Hohe senkt sich nieder,
Als könnte jeder nur am Platz des andern
Befriedigung verworrner Wünsche finden.
der König in *Die natürliche Tochter*, I, 5

Schon im Jahr 1785 hatte die Halsbandgeschichte einen unaussprechlichen Eindruck auf mich gemacht. In dem unsittlichen Stadt-, Hof- und Staats- Abgrunde, der sich hier öffnete, erschienen mir die greulichsten Folgen gespensterhaft. . . .

"Tag- und Jahreshefte," under 1789

Denn leider alles, was zur Sprache kam, machte nur das greuliche Verderben deutlich, worin der Hof und die Vornehmeren befangen lagen.

Kampagne in Frankreich, under October 10, 1792

Ich hasse jeden gewaltsamen Umsturz, weil dabei ebensoviel Gutes vernichtet als gewonnen wird. Ich hasse die, welche ihn ausführen, wie die, welche dazu Ursache geben.

conversation with Eckermann, April 27, 1825

30.

Herrschen und geniessen geht nicht zusammen. Geniessen heisst, sich und andern in Fröhlichkeit angehören; herrschen heisst, sich und andern im ernstlichsten Sinne wohltätig sein.

Hecker, No. 966

Erwerben, Erhalten, Erweitern, Mitteilen, Geniessen gehen gleichen Schrittes und in diesem lebendigen Ebenmass lässt uns die bürgerliche Weisheit ihre schönsten Wirkungen sehen.

Benvenuto Cellini, 1795, Anhang, notes on the early Medicis

Dürfen wir fortfahren, ernsthafter zu sprechen, als es der Gegenstand zu erlauben scheint; so bemerken wir: dass die lebhaftesten und höchsten Vergnügen, wie die vorbeifliegenden Pferde nur einen Augenblick uns erscheinen, uns rühren, und kaum eine Spur in der Seele zurücklassen, dass Freiheit und Gleichheit nur in dem Taumel des Wahnsinns genossen werden können, und dass die grösste Lust nur dann am höchsten reizt, wenn sie sich ganz nahe an die Gefahr drängt, und lüstern ängstlich-süsse Empfindungen in ihrer Nähe geniesset.

Das Römische Carneval, 1789, conclusion

31.

"Was will die Nadel nach Norden gekehrt?"
Sich selbst zu finden, es ist ihr verwehrt.

. . . .

Soll dein Kompass dich richtig leiten,
Hüte dich vor Magnetstein', die dich begleiten.

Hecker, Verse p. 11f

Euer fahles Wesen, schwankende Positur,
Euer Trippeln und Krappeln und Schneidernatur,
Euer ewig lauschend Ohr,
Euer Wunsch, hinten und vorne zu glänzen,
Lernt freilich wie ein armes Rohr
Vor jedem Winde Reverenzen.

Hanswursts Hochzeit, 1775, Paralipomena

Denn der Mensch, der zur schwankenden Zeit auch schwankend
gesinnt ist,
Der vermehret das Übel und breitet es weiter und weiter;
Aber wer fest auf dem Sinne beharrt, der bildet die Welt sich.

Hermann und Dorothea, Urania, conclusion

32.

Wie Natur im Vielgebilde
Einen Gott nur offenbart,
So im weiten Kunstgefilde
Webt ein Sinn der ew'gen Art;
Dieses ist der Sinn der Wahrheit,
Der sich nur mit Schönem schmückt,
Und getrost der höchsten Klarheit
Hellsten Tags entgegenblickt.

Wilhelm Meisters Wanderjahre, II, 8;
first version, 1821, Ch. 13

Freuet euch des wahren Scheins,
Euch des ernsten Spieles:
Kein Lebend'ges ist ein Eins,
Immer ist's ein Vieles!

. . . .

Und es ist das ewig Eine,
Das sich vielfach offenbart:
Klein das Grosse, gross das Kleine,
Alles nach der eignen Art,
Immer wechselnd, fest sich haltend,
Nah und fern und fern und nah,
So gestaltend, umgestaltend —
Zum Erstaunen bin ich da.

Hecker, Verse p. 65f

Das schönste Glück des denkenden Menschen ist, das Erforschliche erforscht zu haben und das Unerforschliche ruhig zu verehren.

Hecker, No. 1207

INDEX OF FIRST LINES

German

English

Bakis reveals to you also the past, for even the bygone	16
Did you behold the wave that rolled in over the seashore?	19
Ever will he be to you the One who does into Many	32
Fond am I of a movable body, ever directed	31
How many apples do you expect from these blossoms? — "One thousand.	25
If the neck of the swan contracts and, with countenance human,	4
Keys are scattered about in the book for solving the riddle,	15
Let me rest, I am sleeping. — "But I am awake." — No, you are not. —	14
Lo, this is it, the highest, and yet it is also the basest;	30
Long and narrow a road. As soon as you walk it, it broadens.	2
Look at the bird. He flies from one tree on to the other,	28
Madness, they said to Calchas, and Madness, they said to Cassandra,	1
Maiden alone at home, with gold and silken adornment,	10
May, when a wandering prince lies down on the wintery threshold,	6
Mice assemble upon the open market. The wand'rer	9
Mighty are you and also refined, all bow to your splendor	12
Not the future alone does Bakis proclaim; what's at present	3
One comes rolling along, the nine are standing there calmly.	24
One I should like to please, so thinks the maiden. The second	20
One thing I know that, upright, is honored, even is worshipped;	29
Pale you appear to me and dead to the eye. How then do you	21
Seven walk enveloped, and seven showing their faces.	7
Tell me, what are you counting? — "I count to determine what ten is,	18
Tell me how to get rid of the sparrows, inquired the gard'ner,	26
Tinkling I hear: it is the merry bells of the sleigh ride.	27
Twice will the hair change color, at first from blond into chestnut,	22
Two I see: the great one, I see the greater. The two will	5
Walls I see that are fallen and walls I see newly erected.	13
When the heavens open and rain, the water will trickle	17
Why then are you affrighted? — "Away, away with these specters,	23
Yes, ye roll from Jupiter, floodtide mightily streaming,	11
Yesterday it was not there, nor will be today or tomorrow.	8

Designed by Gerard A. Valerio

Composed in Linotype Fairfield with
Perpetua display by J. H. Furst Company

Printed letterpress by J. H. Furst Company
on 60 lb. Perkins and Squier RR

Bound by Moore and Co. in Columbia
Riverside Vellum RV-1750